CUMBERLAND'S ARMY

The British Army at Culloden

by
Stuart Reid

PARTIZAN PRESS

Published by Partizan Press 2006
816 - 818 London Road, Leigh-on-sea,
Essex, SS9 3NH
Ph/Fx: +44 (0) 1702 473986
Email: ask@caliverbooks.com
www.caliverbooks.com

First published in Great Britain in 2006 by
Partizan Press

Design & Production by Jay Forster
(www.generate.me.uk)

ISBN: 978-1-85818-529-3

Printed in the UK by Haynes Ltd, Somerset

Front Page:
A member of Captain Duncan Campbell's
company of the 43rd Highlanders (Black Watch)
which fought at Culloden. By Bob Marrion (after
C.C.P. Lawson)
(© Bob Marrion)

Back Page:
British infantry company 1746.
(© Stuart Reid)

OTHER PARTIZAN HISTORICAL TITLES:

CONTENTS

INTRODUCTION

The story of the battle of Culloden has traditionally been told from the Jacobite viewpoint. There are good reasons for this. Romanticism aside there is no doubt that it was one of the decisive moments in Scottish history and more particularly in Highland history. As the late John Prebble pointed out, although the battle did not of itself bring about the destruction of clan society, or even initiate the process, it does dramatically symbolise it's passing. There was however another and rather more practical factor; for those who survived, the Rising was the defining moment in their lives and so they seem to have been compelled to produce a most remarkable body of letters and memoirs describing it at length and in considerable detail. While immensely valuable in itself this body of literature is not matched by anything comparable from the other side and so not only have the Jacobite memoirs tended to set the agenda, but the near total reliance on those sources, and a partisan tendency to erroneously refer to Cumberland's soldiers as Hanoverians, glosses over the fact that Culloden was won by the British Army.

Indeed had the battle of Culloden been fought against the French alone, the gallant stand of Barrell's 4th Foot would rank among one of the British soldier's most desperate fights - indeed for a time the regiment bore *Culloden* as a battle honour. Similarly, while the bloody pursuit by the British cavalry is routinely condemned - that was exactly what cavalry were trained to do. Indeed the irony is all the greater in that Culloden actually ranks as one of the British cavalry's more successful operations.

The purpose of this book is therefore to rescue that British Army from an undeserved obscurity; to describe the army, and also to go some way to describing the battle as it was seen using letters written by British officers and soldiers.

Culloden Moor

In outline the battle of Culloden was a straightforward enough affair which appears to have lasted rather less than an hour. The Duke of Cumberland's intentions were straightforward. He intended to advance to contact with the Jacobite army and fight it where it stood. The immediate tactical planning was equally straightforward. The infantry marched across country in three columns abreast which were intended to deploy into three battle-lines stacked one behind the other. He was aiming in short to have sufficient depth to absorb the impact of a Highland charge. However, as his official report relates, it soon became necessary to modify this and by the time all the preliminary manoeuvring was complete and the first shots exchanged, Cumberland's regular infantry was formed in just two lines at Culloden.

Initially the front line comprised the First and Third Brigades, under the overall command of Lord Albemarle, with 2/1st Royals on the right as befitted their senior status and Barrell's 4th Foot on the extreme left, as the next most senior. Similarly the second line, under Major General John "Daddy" Huske comprised the Second and

Fourth Brigades with Howard's 3rd (Buffs) on the right and Wolfe's 8th Foot on the left.

Small oval portrait of the Duke of Cumberland

It is important to appreciate that, as will be apparent from a number of contemporary accounts, Wolfe's Regiment was *not* posted at right angles to the front of Barrell's Regiment in the front line. Although shown thus in many secondary sources they actually remained in the second line until sent forward during Major General Huske's counter-attack.

Behind this second line was Mordaunt's Fifth Brigade or Reserve, originally three battalions strong, but reduced to just Blakeney's 27th Foot (Inniskillings) since Pulteney's 13th and Battereau's 62nd were used to extend the right of the first and second lines respectively.

London Gazette Extraordinary April 26.
This afternoon arriv'd a Messenger from the Duke of Cumberland, with the following Particulars of the Victory obtain'd by his Royal Highness over the Rebels, on Wednesday the 16th inst. near Culloden.

Inverness April 18, 1746.

On Tuesday the 25th the Rebels burnt Fort Augustus, which convinced us of their Resolution to stand an Engagement with the King's Troops. We gave our Men a Day's Halt at Nairn, and on the 16th march'd from thence, between Four and Five, in four Columns. The three Lines of Foot (reckoning the Reserve for one) were broken into three from the Right, which made the three Columns equal, and each of five Battalions. The Artillery and Baggage followed the first Column upon the Right, and the Cavalry made the fourth Column on the Left.

After we had marched about eight Miles, our advanced Guard, composed of about forty of Kingston's, and the Highlanders led by the Quarter-Master-General, perceived the Rebels at some Distance making a Motion towards us on the Left, upon which we immediately formed; but, finding the Rebels were still a good Way from us, and that the whole Body did not come forward, we put ourselves again upon our March in our former Posture, and continued it to within a Mile of them, where we formed again in the same Order as before. After reconnoitring their Situation, we found them posted behind some old Walls and Huts, in a Line with Culloden House. As we thought our Right entirely Secure, Gen. Hawley and Gen. Bland went to the Left with the two Regiments of Dragoons, to endeavour to fall upon the right Flank of the Rebels, and Kingston's Horse were order'd to the Reserve. The ten Pieces of Cannon were disposed, two in each of the intervals of the first Line, and all our Highlanders (except about 140 which were upon the Left with Gen. Hawley, and who behaved extremely well) were left to guard the Baggage.

When we were advanced within 500 yards of the Rebels, we found the Morass upon our Right was ended, which left our right Flank quite uncover'd to them; his Royal Highness thereupon immediately order'd Kingston's Horse from the Reserve, and a little Squadron of about 60 of Cobham's which had been patrolling, to cover our Flank; and Pulteneys Regiment was order'd from the Reserve to the Right of the Royals.

We spent above half an Hour after that, trying which should gain the Flank of the other; and his Royal Highness having sent Lord Bury forward within 100 Yards of the Rebels, to reconnoitre somewhat that appeared like a Battery to us, they thereupon began firing their Cannon, which was extremely ill serv'd and ill pointed: Ours immediately answer'd them, which began their Confusion. They then came running on in their wild Manner; and upon the Right where his Royal Highness had plac'd himself, imagining the greatest Push would be there, they came down three several Times within 100 Yards of our Men, firing their Pistols and brandishing their swords; but the Royals and Pulteney's hardly took their Firelocks from their Shoulders, so that after these faint Attempts they made off; and the little Squadrons on our Right were sent to pursue them. Gen. Hawley had, by the Help of our Highlanders, beat down two little Stone Walls, and came in upon the right Flank of their second Line.

As their whole first Line came down to attack at once, their Right somewhat outflanked Barrel's Regiment, which was our Left, and the greatest Part of the little Loss we sustain'd was there; but Bligh's and Sempil's giving a Fire upon those who had out-flank'd Barrels, soon repulsed them, and Barrel's Regiment and the left of Monro's fairly beat them with their Bayonets: There was scarce a Soldier or Officer of Barrel's, and of that Part of Monro's which engaged, who did not kill one or two Men each with their Bayonets and Spontoons.

The Cavalry, which had charged from Right and Left, met in the center, except two Squadrons of Dragoons, which we missed, and they were gone in Pursuit of the Runaways: Lord Ancram was order'd to pursue with the Horse as he could; and did it with so good Effect, that a very considerable Number was kill'd in the Pursuit.

As we were in our March to Inverness, and were near arriv'd there, Major General Bland sent the annexed Papers [not included] which he receiv'd from the French Officers and Soldiers surrendering themselves Prisoners, to his Royal Highness. Maj. Gen. Bland had also made great Slaughter, and took about 50 French Officers and Soldiers Prisoners in his Pursuit.

By the best Calculation that can be made, 'tis thought the Rebels lost 2000 Men upon the Field of Battle, and in the Pursuit. We have here 222 French, and 326 Rebel Prisoners, as will appear by Lists hereunto annexed. [not included] Lieut. Col. Howard killed an Officer, who appeared to be Lord Strathallan, by the seal and different Commissions from the Pretender found in his Pocket.

Other accounts

So far as possible less official accounts of the battle are filed according to regiment. The majority, however, tended to simply appear in newspapers credited to "an officer", and some of these are given below:

Extract from a Letter from an Officer at Inverness, dated April 19.[1]

On the 16th inst. on Drummossie Moor, the Rebels had posted themselves to very great Advantage, having inclosed Fields to their Right and Left, with Stone Walls for the Foot to fire over, and their Flank and Centre strengthened with Cannon; which they kept firing constantly before ours were ready, tho' no Time was lost on our Side, the Duke giving all his Orders with the greatest Coolness imaginable, and a Smile on his Countenance the whole Time. Ld Albemarle and all the Generals behaved well, as did all the Soldiers on that glorious Day, in which 9000 Rebels, with all the above Advantages, were entirely defeated by about 6000 of the King's Forces. The Clans are quite dispersed, the Pretender has dismissed his Guard, taken the white Cockade out of his Cap, and given all up as lost to him.

We expect soon to march into the Highlands after them, and then send the Campbells, Loudoon's, grants &c. in pursuit of the scatter'd Remains of a daring set of Villains, who were once come to a great Head, but are now as much dejected as possible, there remaining with them no Money, or Ammunition, few Arms, or Chiefs of Clans, and most of their daring Men are on the Ground at Culloden.

Extract of a Letter from Inverness dated April 16.[2]

As soon as we saw the Rebel Army, we form'd and march'd towards them in Order of Battle, more than two Miles till we came within 500 Yards of them. After Cannonading a little on their Side, they gave us two rounds of Small arms and advanced towards us; but when they were within 200 Yards of us, our Cannon fired Grape Shot upon them, till they were close upon us. Our Front Line gave them several Fires which made them retire in a great Hurry. The Horse and Dragoons were ordered to fall on their Flanks; which they did with a great Fury. Our Infantry mov'd after them in Order and kept a continual Fire upon them. His Royal Highness the Duke was in the Front Line all the time of the Action, several Shot were aimed at him, but missed him, thank God. 'Tis certain the Rebels were equal in Number to us. We had 10 Three pounders drawn up in the Front Line, and six small Mortars.

1 *Newcastle Journal* - the unusual reference to Drummossie Moor suggests that the writer had some local knowledge.
2 Newcastle Courant

The British Army in 1746

Organisation

The British Army at Culloden comprised 16 regiments of infantry, three regiments of cavalry, and one company of artillery.

Although they are all too commonly referred to as Hanoverian soldiers, they were nothing of the sort. King George's Hanoverian soldiers were in Germany, where they belonged. Those who fought at Culloden were *British* soldiers. In fact four out of Cumberland's sixteen infantry battalions at Culloden were Scottish regiments and as will be seen there were a surprising number of Scots officers and soldiers standing in the ranks of what are now regarded English regiments. In fact the only casualty returned by Wolfe's 8th Foot was a newly commissioned Ensign Robert Bruce!

In character it was also a rather familiar army. Most of its recruits were either agricultural labourers keen to see a bit of the world rather than working themselves to death in the parish of their birth or equally discontented weavers and other cloth-workers. Other trades were also represented of course, but between them the countrymen and the weavers accounted for most of King George's soldiers. It is easy to dwell upon the hardships of a soldier's life, and to emphasise the supposedly harsh discipline, but there was no denying its very real compensations: soldiers were properly and regularly clothed and fed and if their pay was low at least it was constant - unlike in civilian life. Moreover, when not actually on active service soldiers could supplement the King's pay by taking on casual work in their spare time - of which they had a surprising amount.

Ordinarily they enlisted for unlimited service which usually meant being discharged in their 40s, although at least one soldier at Culloden, Private John Tovey of Monro's 37th Foot was all of 59 when he had his jaw shot away. There was no automatic entitlement to a pension, unless of course a man was disabled in the service, for the government took the robust view that if a man was capable of earning his living he had no need of a pension. In true 18th century style however this seemingly callous attitude was relieved in practice by the remarkable frequency with which those men discharged after 20 years good service were granted disability pensions on the rather loose grounds of being 'worn out'.

Nevertheless, a few of the soldiers who served at Culloden were not volunteers. In 1745 two acts were rushed through Parliament encouraging magistrates to conscript "all able-bodied men who do not follow or exercise any lawful calling or employment". For each reluctant recruit thus delivered up the parish constables received a bounty of £3 paid into the vestry account, hence their informal designation as Vestry Men. The Army was actually quite choosy about where it found its recruits and so viewed these conscripts with a distinctly jaundiced eye. They were therefore allotted all the dirty jobs such as battlefield clearance and burial details - and although they were discharged as soon as possible after the battle, it was these men who were set to guarding the Jacobite prisoners with results which were as unhappy as they were predictable.

Normally regular infantry regiments comprised a single battalion of 10 companies, one of which was designated as grenadiers, but in wartime it was common for one or more "additional companies" to be authorised which were not intended to be combat units, but served as a regimental depot. This did not always work out in practice since the two companies of the 1st (Royals) captured in the affair at High Bridge were additional companies which had been hastily pressed into service as the only troops available to reinforce Fort William at short notice, and the Black Watch unit which fought at Culloden was also an additional company.

Each company was normally led by a captain, although three of them also doubled up as what were termed field officers, ie; the colonel, lieutenant colonel and major. On a day to day basis therefore their companies were actually commanded by lieutenants and in the case of the colonel's company his frequent absence on other duties meant that his lieutenant was dignified by the curious title of captain-lieutenant and ranked socially as the junior captain rather than the senior lieutenant. Ordinarily the junior officers in each company comprised a lieutenant and an ensign, but the grenadier company, which in action was divided into two platoons and posted on the flanks of the regiment, had a second lieutenant in place of the ensign. A number of regiments, including the 1st (Royal) Regiment also had additional or second lieutenants serving with the ordinary "battalion "companies, as a wartime augmentation.

The regimental staff comprised four commissioned officers; the adjutant, who acted as an assistant to the major and looked after most routine administration. The quartermaster was primarily responsible for the battalion's "quarters", which could be a camp ground, a billet or a garrison. He would also, generally speaking, be responsible for route planning on marches, and looking after the regimental baggage train. He was not, at this period, directly responsible for supplies. Both officers might hold also hold line commissions as ensigns or lieutenants in addition to these staff appointments. The surgeon, who also sometimes held a line commission, by way of boosting his pay, was of course the battalion's medical officer and was assisted by a Mate, who was not a commissioned officer, while the fourth staff officer was the Chaplain, who did hold the King's commission but rarely if ever appeared at headquarters let alone hold services.

Cavalry regiments had a similar command structure, but only mustered six companies rather than ten, which were designated as troops. In action the troops would normally be paired off to form three squadrons, although Kingston's 10th Horse, which may only have mustered about 200 troopers, was formed in just two squadrons at Culloden.

Uniforms

Soldiers' clothing and equipment of the time was both practical and comfortable; comprising a red double-breasted greatcoat, worn over a long-skirted waistcoat which was really an under-jacket or tunic, knee breeches, canvas gaiters to protect the legs from mud (and heather) and a tricorne hat trimmed with lace which metamorphosed on campaign into broad-brimmed slouch hat. The lapels so prominently displayed in the illustrations of the time were normally buttoned across on active service, especially in inclement weather and the coat skirts were also unhooked as seen in the Penicuik sketches. All in all it was not a bad outfit for a winter campaign in rough country. Their personal equipment included a 46" barrelled Long Land Pattern firelock and bayonet, a light sword or hanger (if it had not been 'lost') and all the usual impedimenta of knapsack, haversack and canteen required by all soldiers, rebel or regular.

Cavalrymen were similarly clothed and equipped with the obvious difference that heavy jacked leather boots were substituted for the gaiters, and broadswords for hangers. The carbines carried by cavalrymen were not noticeably shorter than infantry muskets since they had a barrel length of 42". Other differences included a lack of turned back lapels on the coats (which were nevertheless cut to be double-breasted) and very thin or no lace, and most strikingly, the wearing of waistcoats and breeches in the regimental facing colour, rather than the plain red ones worn by most infantry units.

Regiments were distinguished one from another in two ways. The first was by means of the facing colour, used to line the coats. Blue was reserved for royal regiments and most others made do with either yellow, buff or green, though there was quite a variation in the exact shade used. Nevertheless, as it was clearly necessary to distinguish between two regiments displaying the same facing colour, a system of decorative lacing had evolved. The lace was actually a worsted tape, almost invariably white, with a pattern of coloured lines, zig-zags or other designs unique to the

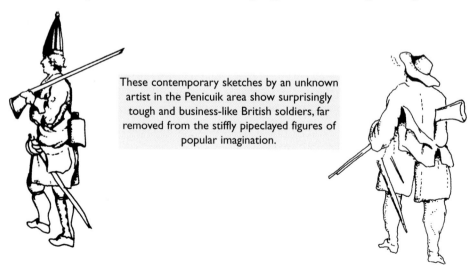

These contemporary sketches by an unknown artist in the Penicuik area show surprisingly tough and business-like British soldiers, far removed from the stiffly pipeclayed figures of popular imagination.

regiment woven into it. This 'lace' was used to edge coats and button-holes and also appeared on the sleeves, usually in a ladder pattern although some regiments preferred a herring-bone arrangement.

The regiment's grenadier company, made up of the oldest and steadiest men, was also distinguished by the wearing of a pointed mitre cap. This had originally begun as a simple stocking cap but by this period had acquired a stiffened front in the regimental facing colour. Royal regiments, and certain "old" corps, such as the Inniskillings were permitted to wear embroidered badges on the front, while less exalted units made do with the royal cipher.

All of these distinctions are discussed in greater detail in the individual regimental entries.

Infantry Fighting Tactics

The British Army's basic tactical philosophy amounted to forming up in a line, three men deep, and blazing away until fire superiority was achieved and the enemy ran away. This depended on being able to maintain a steady rolling fire and the chosen method of delivering that fire was 'Platooning' as laid down in the official 1728 *Regulations*. This battle drill required a battalion to be divided into a series of *ad hoc* platoons each of between 20-30 men who would fire in a pre-arranged sequence rippling up and down the line. With practice, it was possible for soldiers to loose off four or even five rounds a minute, but under stress soldiers will always fire high and this rate of fire was not only wasteful but quite unsustainable since it was common to go into action with as few as 12 rounds a man. Instead officers and NCOs controlled the firing, holding it down to a rate of two or at most three rounds per minute, so that the men remained cool and levelled their firelocks properly instead of shooting rapidly into the air. Despite its limitations the tactic of Platooning was therefore effective enough in conventional operations, especially against the French whose fire discipline was notoriously bad, but employing it against Highlanders simply did not work. The deliberately paced rate of fire, while well adapted to maintaining a sustained firefight, simply could not kill enough clansmen quickly enough to stop a determined, fast-moving Highland charge.

A change of tactics was called for and at Culloden heavy massed battalion volleys were employed instead. There was an obvious danger that if the volley was badly timed, the whole battalion might still be frantically reloading as the charge came in. The answer, therefore, was to direct the front rank not to reload after that first volley, but instead to charge their bayonets as soon as they had fired, thus protecting the second and third ranks as *they* reloaded and poured in a succession of volleys at point blank range.

Surviving grenadier cap of the period. The main part of the front was in the regimental facing colour, with the GR cypher embroidered in the lace colour and the crown in full colour. The "little flap", bearing the white horse of Hanover and the motto Nec Aspera Terrent was red., as was the rear of the cap. (S Reid)

Infantry Regiments

The Culloden regiments appear below as organised in brigades on the day of the battle. Ordinarily at this time they were referred to simply by the name of the colonel, for the regiment quite literally belonged to him. He, ultimately approved (or disapproved) all promotions and drew all manner of financial perquisites from it and the closeness of the interest he took in its welfare did much to set the regimental 'tone'. As will be starkly obvious from the lists below Scottish commanding officers for example frequently used their patronage to bring other Scottish officers into regiments normally regarded as 'English'. It was common, however, not only for the names of commanding officers to change as the older ones died, but sometimes officers might be shifted from regiment to regiment, perhaps to take a poor unit in hand or simply to 'promote' an officer to the command of a more senior regiment. Thus Lord Sempill had once commanded the 43rd/42nd Black Watch, but at Culloden had moved on to take command of the 25th (Edinburgh) Regiment - later the King's Own Scottish Borderers. To avoid the obvious confusion which this sort of thing could lead to, numbers were assigned to regiments supposedly reflecting their seniority within the army, although they would not be ordered to be placed upon regimental colours and drums until 1747 and did not definitely take precedence over the colonel's names until 1751.

All officers carried on their regiments' books on 16 April 1746[1] are listed below in order of their seniority by commission date within the regiment. A number of units had suffered heavy casualties amongst their officers at Falkirk on 17 January 1746 and those killed there are also included, but distinguished by italics.

It will be obvious from the figures in Cumberland's morning state that not all of the living officers listed were actually present at Culloden. Most regimental colonels were of course general officers, while others served as governors of fortresses or merely enjoyed a semi-retirement. Less exalted officers like Captain John Crosbie of the 21st might be commanding detachments, or holding general staff appointments or were on sick leave, or even in some cases had not yet joined their units for one reason or another.

A similar uncertainty surrounds the rank and file. Two quite separate and in some degree contradictory sets of figures survive setting out the number of officers and men serving in each regiment. The first and what should be the most accurate is Cumberland's morning state for 16 April 1746 which quite literally lists the actual numbers of officers and men actually present and fit for duty in each of the 15 regiments of regular infantry at roll call that morning.

The so-called "Guildhall List" on the other hand, recording the sums of money distributed to those same regiments from a charitable fund established by London's Guildhall does not include the officers, and the figures for the rank and file are generally quite markedly higher. An immediate and obvious difference lies in the fact that the Guildhall figures include some 20-30 corporals in each regiment. As no corporals are separately mentioned in the morning state it is unclear whether they were omitted from it in error or are actually included within the figures for the rank and file.

That question aside, the answer to the apparent discrepancies lies in the fact that the morning state only records those men actually standing in the ranks, fit for duty, and omits the very considerable number of men who were sick or otherwise absent - such as the detachments at Aberdeen and Blair. In late March for example Major John LaFausille of the 8th Foot was reportedly en route to Aberdeen with as many as 500 recruits and recovered sick men, but did not catch up with the army before the battle was fought. Others perhaps were indeed present but were still left out of battle for some reason, such as the new recruits and the vestry men (semi-criminal conscripts levied for the duration of the emergency), who were assigned instead to look after the baggage. Since all of these men, whether with Major Fausille or not, were entered on their regiments' books on the day of the action they qualified for the Guildhall bounty even although they were not actually standing in the firing line.

FIRST BRIGADE

In this brigade, as with the others the most senior regiment stood on the right, the next in seniority on the left and the junior regiment in the centre. Thus it was deployed with 2/1st (Royal) on the right, then 34th Foot in the centre and 14th Foot on the left.

2/1st (Royal) Regiment

Facing colour: Blue, with gold lace for officers and plain white lace for the rank and file. Button-hole loops were pointed according to the 1742 *Cloathing Book* but square ended by the time David Morier painted them c1748. The former shows no lace on the sleeves, while Morier depicts the common 'ladder' pattern. Grenadier caps bore a GR cipher on a blue roundel with the green collar of St. Andrew, bearing *Nemo Me Impune Lacessit* in yellow. As a Royal regiment it was entitled to wear blue breeches in place of the usual red.

Better known as the Royal Scots, this regiment, the oldest in the British Army, was unusual in that it had two battalions; of which only the Second, recalled from garrison duty in Ireland fought at Falkirk and Culloden. The fact that so many officers' commissions date from 1742 is a reflection of the heavy losses suffered by the regiment while serving in the Caribbean shortly before.

Colonel
Hon. James St.Clair   26 Jun 1737   Lieut.General - not present

Lieut.Colonel
John Ramsay   12 Mar 1742

Major
James Forrester   20 Apr 1742

2/1st (Royal) Regiment - The Cloathing Book 1742
(Private collection.)

Captains

Claudius Fraser	7 Sep 1741	James Faviere	5 Apr 1742
James Hay	17 Apr 1742	William Cunningham	20 Apr 1742
Frederick Hamilton	7 Sep 1742	David Dickson	22 Feb 1743
Sir Henry Erskine Bt.	12 Mar 1743[2]	William Craufurd	1 May 1744

Lieutenants

Alexander Hay	24 Apr 1742	William Montgomery	1 Mar 1742
John Innes	7 Mar 1742*	William Young	9 Mar 1742**
James Masterson	10 Mar 1742	Patrick Gordon	1 Apr 1742
James Cunningham	14 Apr 1742	Robert Gordon	1 May 1742
Thomas Ogle	25 May 1742	Robert Mirrie	22 June 1742
James Buchannan	13 Nov 1744	Gilbert McAdam	26 Sep 1745

* Quartermaster 23 Oct 1745
** Died 23 Apr 1746

Second Lieutenants

Robert Vicars	16 May 1742	Francis Folliott	18 May 1742
Alexander McKenzie	19 May 1742*	Alexander Denham	22 May 1742
Henry Oswald	9 Jun 1744	James Bruce	15 Oct 1744
Philip Skene	26 Sep 1745	John Murray	29 Nov 1745

* posted to 1st Bn 19 Apr 1746

Ensigns

John Buchannan	26 Feb 1742	Walter Campbell	2 Apr 1742
Obadiah Bourne	1 May 1744	James Dalrymple	2 May 1744
John McKay	9 Jun 1744	James Spital	25 Oct 1744
John Steuart	1 Jun 1745	William, Lord Strathnavar	29 Nov 1745
William Hawkins	29 Nov 1745		

Adjutant	Alexander Sinclair	11 Jun 1744
Surgeon	John McColme	1 May 1744
Chaplain	John Lloyd	1 Sep 1741

NB: since the colonel's company was part of the First Battalion there were eight captains' companies in the Second Battalion and consequently no captain lieutenant.

According to the morning state 2 field officers, 5 captains, 19 subalterns, 29 sergeants, 25 drummers and 401 rank and file were actually present for duty. The Guildhall List on the other hand evidences 30 sergeants, 37 corporals, 26 drummers and 420 privates. Corporals aside this represents a discrepancy of one sergeant, one drummer and 19 men.

Of those who were certainly present at Culloden, four men were returned as wounded and three of them subsequently obtained pensions:

Alexander Buchannan, aged 24, was disabled in the left leg.
John Reynolds, aged 44, was similarly wounded in the left knee.
John Ross, aged 33, was "disabled by a rupture at Culloden".

Pulteney's 13th Foot 1746 *Charge your bayonets.* (S Reid)

Pulteney's 13th Foot 1746 *Push your bayonets.* (S Reid)

Regimental Colour (top) and King's Colour (bottom), 2nd Battalion, Royal Scots
(by Lesley Prince)

Royal Artillery Gunner 1748 (Great Britain)
by Bob Marrion (after contemporary painting by Morier at Roermond)

(© Bob Marrion)

A trooper of Cumberland's 15th Dragoons 1748
by Bob Marrion (after David Morier)
This regiment fought at Culloden as Kingston's 10th Horse. Although this would have
been largely the uniform worn at the battle the minor details, facing colours etc are by
no means certain.
(© Bob Marrion)

The circumstances in which John Ross was injured were not explained but it was most likely in assisting to heave some of the artillery pieces out of some boggy ground on the British right wing just before the battle began.

Private Alexander Taylor
It was a very cold rainy Morning, and nothing to buy to comfort us. But we had the Ammunition loaf, thank God; but not a Dram of Brandy or Spirits had you given a Crown for a Gill, nor nothing but the Loaf and Water. We also had great difficulty in keeping the Locks of our Firelocks dry; which was very necessary, for the Day was stormy and the Rain violent... The Battle began by Cannonading, and continued for Half an Hour or more with Great Guns. But our Gunners galling their Lines, they betook themselves to their small Arms, Sword and Pistol, and came running on our Front Line like Troops of Hungry Wolves, and fought with Intrepidity.

Cholmondley's 34th Regiment

Facing colour: Bright Yellow, with silver lace for officers. Other ranks had white lace with a curious design like blue blades of grass in 1742, replaced by a blue scroll and yellow line by 1748. No button-hole loops are shown in the *Cloathing Book* but square-ended ones had been adopted by 1748.

Colonel
Hon. James Cholmondley	18 Dec 1742	Brigadier - not present	

Lieut.Colonel
Maurice Powell	*12 Aug 1741**	Charles Jeffreys	17 Feb 1746**

* Killed at Falkirk 17 Jan 1746
** From 62nd Foot

Major
James Lockhart	25 Oct 1744³

Captains
John Lovell	28 Aug 1737	Edward Webster	1 Jun 1739
Henry Hart	12 Apr 1741	John Lind	12 Apr 1741
Maysmore Maurice	25 Jun 1744	Sir Hugh Williams Bt.	26 Jun 1744
Hon. Robert Monckton	27 Jun 1744	Balthazar Trapaud	25 Oct 1744
Cranfield S. Powell	22 Apr 1745		

Capt. Lieutenant
Hezekiah Fleming	17 Mar 1744	Brevet Major	27 Sep 1745

Lieutenants
Charles Terrott	19 Dec 1735	James Hamilton	15 Dec 1738
John Dundas	2 Mar 1739	George Mackay	6 Oct 1742
William Courtenay	28 Sep 1743	David Melville	28 Sep 1743
Michael Alcock	25 Jun 1744	James Hargraves	11 Mar 1745*
Henry Brownrigg	22 Apr 1745	Nehemiah Donellan	1 May 1745
John Collins	1 Dec 1745	William Stacey	2 Dec 1745

* Adjutant 19 Apr 1742

Cholmondley's 34th Regiment -
Victorian reworking of an image in The Cloathing Book 1742
(Private collection.)

Ensigns

Joseph Widdens	26 Mar 1744*	William Hoby	25 Jun 1744
Abraham Hoskins	25 Jun 1744	Woodward Beazeley	25 Oct 1744
Samuel Exley	25 Oct 1744	Cooke Reynell	11 Mar 1745
Charles Long	4 Apr 1745	Walter Burroughs	22 Apr 1745
Thomas Kennan	1 Dec 1745	Alexander Barker	2 Dec 1745
Robert Wilkie	25 Feb 1746		

* Quartermaster   14 Mar 1746

Surgeon	Michael Giles	15 May 1732
Chaplain	Frederick Cornwallis	25 Mar 1738

Another strong regiment mustering 2 field officers, 7 captains, 15 subalterns, 21 sergeants, 15 drummers and 399 rank and file according to the morning state, and 22 sergeants, 24 corporals, 15 drummers and 433 privates in the Guildhall list.

One man was returned as killed and 2 wounded, neither of whom appear in the Chelsea records.

Price's 14th Regiment

Facing colour: Yellowish-Buff, with silver lace for officers. The 1742 *Cloathing Book* shows no lace, but Morier evidences white lace with a blue zig-zag between blue and white stripes, arranged in square ended loops at the button-holes and a ladder pattern on the sleeves.

Colonel

John Price	22 Jun 1743	Brigadier General - not present

Lieut.Colonel

Edward Jeffreys	*12 Sep 1745**	John Grey	17 Feb 1746

* Killed at Falkirk 17 Jan 1746

Major

George Heighington	22 Jun 1745

Captains

Andrew Simpson	11 Mar 1736*	Mark Renton	11 Feb 1741
John Bell	23 Mar 1743	Alexander Grossett	20 Jul 1744**
Edward Booth	1 Aug 1744	John Meard	1 Aug 1744
Richard Russell	22 Jun 1745		

* Died of wounds 23 April 1746
** Killed at Culloden

Capt. Lieutenant

Stringer Lawrence	22 Jun 1745

Lieutenants

James Gabriel Montresor	23 Jul 1737	Bartholomew Corneille	19 Jan 1740
Thomas Bowyer	24 Jan 1741*	William Aitken	23 Mar 1743
Thomas Baylies	20 Jul 1744	George James Bruere	1 Aug 1744
William Price	31 Aug 1744	Francis Lind	22 Jul 1745**
Jonathan Furlong	8 Aug 1745***	John Heighington	1 Dec 1745

* Adjutant 22 Mar 1744
** Surgeon 3 May 1726
*** Q/master 25 Apr 1744

Ensigns

Robert Gordon	11 Jul 1741	Charles Graeme	23 Mar 1743
William Browning	29 Sep 1743	Thomas Lawson	20 Jul 1744
Robert Richard Maitland	1 Aug 1744	John Deaken	22 Jun 1745
( ) Hales	8 Aug 1745	Hammond Clement	1 Dec 1745
Robert Price	1 Dec 1745		

Chaplain
James Armand   22 May 1730

This battalion had 2 field officers, 7 captains, 14 subalterns, 21 sergeants, 11 drummers and 304 rank and file at Culloden according to the morning state, while the Guildhall schedule listed 22 sergeants, 22 corporals, 12 drummers and 339 privates.

Only one man was returned as killed - probably Captain Alexander Grossett, who was murdered by a prisoner while serving on the staff, and 9 wounded, of whom;

> Richard Dennison, lost his left leg
> John Ross, was "wounded in the right ankle"

SECOND BRIGADE

Howard's 3rd Regiment (Buffs)

Facing colour: Light Buff with silver lace for officers and white lace with a yellow line and red chain for rank and file, according to the 1742 *Cloathing Book* although the Morier painting of c.1748 shows white with black/red/yellow edging. Square ended button-hole loops, with a herringbone pattern on the sleeves and coat-skirts in 1742, but pointed ended loops and a ladder pattern on the sleeves by 1748. Grenadier cap had a green dragon.

Colonel
Thomas Howard	27 Jun 1737	Lieut.General - not present

Lieut.Colonel
Sir George Howard	2 Apr 1744

Major
Gerard Elrington	10 Feb 1741

Captains
Cyrus Trapaud	31 Mar 1743	Rowland Hacker	9 Jun 1744
William Cosby	25 Jun 1744	William Nugent	26 Jun 1744
John Barlow	22 Feb 1745	Samuel Criche	29 Nov 1745
Sir John Milne Bt.	29 Nov 1745	Shuckburgh Hewett	18 Jan 1746
John Collet Mawhood	3 Feb 1746		

Capt. Lieutenant
Thomas Jocelyn	18 Jan 1746

Lieutenants
John Barford	26 Mar 1744	Charles Prissick	26 Mar 1744
Francis Stott	2 Apr 1744	Arthur Kennedy	3 Apr 1744
Christopher Teesdale	9 Jun 1744	Richard Henry Roper	25 Jun 1744
Nathaniel Tanner	25 Jun 1744	Robert Aston	21 Nov 1744
William Wright	22 Feb 1745	James Johnston	29 Nov 1745
Thomas Winship	29 Nov 1745	John Biddulph	18 Jan 1746

Ensigns
Barnaby More	*2 Apr 1744**	John Laverock	10 Jun 1744
Thomas Benson	25 Jun 1744	George Nicholson	25 Jun 1744
Edward Pauncefort	20 Nov 1744	Phineas Pett	22 Feb 1745
Henry Trelawney	13 Sep 1745	Thomas Wayne	30 Nov 1745
Francis Paul	1 Dec 1745	Malby Brabazon	18 Jan 1746
Roger Crowle	31 Jan 1746	James French	30 Mar 1746**

* died 31 January 1746
**probably not yet joined

Adjutant	Thomas Ferguson	1 May 1745
Quartermaster	Joseph Wright	1 May 1745
Surgeon	Archibald Johnson	15 Mar 1734
Chaplain	Richard Hughes	27 May 1742

Howard's 3rd Regiment (Buffs) - The Cloathing Book 1742
(Private collection.)

The morning state evidences 2 field officers, 4 captains, 10 subalterns, 21 sergeants, 14 drummers and 413 rank and file actually present and fit for duty, while the Guildhall list gives 24 sergeants, 23 corporals, 16 drummers and no fewer than 493 privates.

One man was returned as killed and two wounded; one of whom was Charles Appleton, 30 years old, disabled in the right hand at Culloden.

Anonymous Sergeant, April 18[4]

We have obtain'd a great and glorious Victory over the Rebels; who, I must own, behaved with the greatest Resolution, to their Cost: but I am sure that Men never were repulsed with so much Vigour as they were: For the Battle began precisely a Quarter after Twelve, and lasted only till One; in which Time our Army killed between 2 and 3000 of the Rebels, besides Numbers coming in wounded; and our killed and wounded does not exceed 150 Men. We have taken Prisoners all the French Officers and Soldiers that were not killed in the Action, and the pretended French Ambassador. We have also taken the Pretender's Coach and Baggage, his Plate, and all his Kitchen Furniture, made in London; with above 200 chests of Arms, 18 Pieces of Cannon, and all the Utinsils belonging to them; which makes the Victory compleat, and will render the Rebels unable to give us Battle again, or disturb his Majesty's Dominions.

Fleming's 36th Regiment

Facing colour: Green, shown as sea-green (bluish) in 1742, but much deeper by 1748. Officers had silver lace, while Other Ranks had white with a green chain in 1742 and a single green line by 1748. No button-hole loops are shown in the *Cloathing Book* but square ended ones had been adopted by 1748. Sleeve lace was arranged in a ladder pattern at both dates.

Colonel
James Fleming	5 Feb 1741	Brigadier - not present

Lieut.Colonel
George Jackson	19 Mar 1745

Major
Robert Browne	19 Mar 1745*	John Petre	17 Feb 1746

* Died of wounds 30 Jan 1746

Captains
Edward Whitmore	1 Nov 1739	Hamilton Lambart	1 Jun 1742
Robert Chamier	25 Jun 1744	William Denny	26 Jun 1744
Hon. Archibald Montgomerie	16 Oct 1744	Hugh Morgan	20 Feb 1745
William Arnot	19 Mar 1745	Gervas Remington	11 Apr 1745
Gilbert Dodd	17 Feb 1746		

Capt. Lieutenant
Henry Gore	17 Feb 1746

Lieutenants

Robert Ackland	1 Jun 1742*	Duncan Brodie	28 Sep 1743
Thomas Maule	18 May 1744	John Fleming	24 Jun 1744
Charles Forbes	25 Jun 1744	Paul Moreau	24 Sep 1744
William Dudley	11 Apr 1745	Dudley Ackland	8 Jul 1745
John Fleming	10 Jul 1745	Samuel Buck Veale	30 Nov 1745
Andrew Napier	17 Feb 1746**	Thomas Buckston	5 Mar 1746

* Surgeon	1 Jul 1734
** Adjutant	16 Nov 1745

Ensigns

Henry Vaughan	25 Jun 1744	George Sheyne	24 Sep 1744
John Foxon	11 Apr 1745	Alexander Duncan	8 Jul 1745
Thomas Elrington	9 Jul 1745	John Mathews	10 Jul 1745
John Price	17 Feb 1746	Blachford Stronge	17 Feb 1746
Robert Hamilton	17 Feb 1746	Humphrey Carleton	25 Feb 1746
George Potter	21 Mar 1746*		

* Probably not yet joined

Quartermaster	John Slocombe	26 Feb 1746
Chaplain	Richard Ward	13 Jan 1743

This regiment had 2 field officers, 6 captains, 18 subalterns, 25 sergeants, 14 drummers and 350 rank and file present on the field, although the Guildhall list evidences 26 sergeants, 22 corporals, 14 drummers and 376 privates.

Six men were returned as wounded, probably by Jacobite artillery fire.

Bligh's 20th Regiment

Facing colour: Yellow, with silver lace for officers. The 1742 *Cloathing Book* shows a rather old-fashioned single-breasted coat with plain white lace. However lapels were ordered for all regiments lacking them in 1743 and Morier shows white lace edged black on both sides, with two red stripes. Button loops were square ended and the sleeve lace was arranged in ladder pattern.

Colonel

Thomas Bligh	16 Dec 1740	Brigadier General - not present

Lieut.Colonel

Hon. Edward Cornwallis	27 May 1745

Major

Anthony Meyrac	27 May 1745

Captains

Cromwell Ward	26 Aug 1737*	John Williams	13 May 1742
Robert Hart	18 Sep 1743	John Milburne	25 Jun 1744
Sheldon Walter	26 Jun 1744	Lewis La Bouchetiere	29 May 1745
George Townshend	29 May 1745**	James Ashe	28 Jun 1745
Daniel Robertson	22 Aug 1745		

* Town Major of Carlisle
** Cumberland's staff

Capt. Lieutenant

John Vickers	22 Aug 1745

Lieutenants

John Beckwith	1 Jul 1740★	Alexander Trapaud	10 Mar 1743
Thomas Dalton	18 Sep 1743	Walter Johnstone	18 Sep 1743
Charles Teate O'Hara	4 Oct 1743	William Billing	25 Jun 1744
James Hartley	28 Jun 1745	Thomas W. Lawrence	28 Jun 1745
Thomas Parsons	28 Jun 1745	John Slowe	28 Jun 1745
William Robinson	22 Aug 1745	Edward Crymble	30 Nov 1745

★ Adjutant 10 Oct 1745
★★ Wounded at Culloden

Ensigns

Samuel Crocker	4 Oct 1743	John Maxwell	25 Apr 1745
Joseph Frearson	29 May 1745	Peter Hennis	29 May 1745
Alexander Tennant	28 Jun 1745	John Parr	28 Jun 1745
Alexander McDowell	28 Jun 1745	Thomas Clements	22 Aug 1745
William Marshall	14 Oct 1745	John Gunn	30 Nov 1745

Quartermaster	William Parsons	25 Apr 1742
Surgeon	George Corryn	17 Apr 1732
Chaplain	Israel Bataille	-

The morning state lists 2 field officers, 5 captains, 13 subalterns, 22 sergeants, 13 drummers and 412 rank and file. The Guildhall figures are 23 sergeants, 25 corporals, 14 drummers and 464 privates.

Four men were killed and 17 wounded, including;

> Corporal George Fowkes, from Dublin, disabled in the right leg
> John Bynam, disabled by a wound in his right foot
> Joseph Simmers, wounded in his head
> Archibald Smith, shot in the mouth and wounded in the side
> Robert Spence, lost his right arm

Volunteer Michael Hughes:

We marched on a mile or two before we could discern the terrible boasting Highlanders, and upon first sight of them we formed into line of action, which was done with great beauty of discipline and order. We marched up to our knees in water over a bog that brought us in perfect sight of them. We kept advancing with drums beating and colours flying, with fixed bayonets till we came within gunshot. We then halted a little for the boggy ground hindered the bringing up of our cannon... Making a dreadful huzza, and even crying "Run, ye dogs!", they broke in between the grenadiers of Barrel and Monro; but these had given their fire according to the general direction, and then parried them with their screwed bayonets. The two cannon on that division were so well served, that when within two yards of them they received a full discharge of cartridge shot, which made a dreadful havoc; and those who crowded into the opening received a full fire from the centre of Bligh's regiment, which still increased the number of the slain. However, such as survived possessed themselves of the cannon, and attacked the regiments sword in hand; but to their astonishment they found an obstinate resistance. It was dreadful to see the enemies' swords circling in the air as they were raised from strokes, and no less to see the officers of the Army, some cutting with their swords, others pushing with their spontoons, the Serjeants running their halberds into the throats of the enemy, while the soldiers mutually defended each other, and pirced the Heart of his Opponent, ramming their bayonets up to the socket. But still more terrible to hear the dying groans of either party.

Barrell's 4th Regiment

Facing colour: Blue, perhaps with gold lace for officers although definitely wearing silver when David Morier painted his famous *Incident in the Rebellion* c.1753. Other ranks lace was white with a blue zig-zag, with square ended loops and a ladder pattern on the sleeves. There was no alteration between 1742 and 1748, but the 1753 painting shows that by then it had altered to a herringbone pattern on the sleeves. The grenadier cap bore a GR cipher on a red roundel within a blue garter bearing the motto *Honi Soi Qui Mal y pense* in white.

Interestingly, in view of the role played by this regiment in the battle, it appears to have had a higher than normal proportion of Scots officers, including Ensign John Brown, badly wounded while carrying the colours.[5]

Colonel
William Barrell	8 Aug 1734	Lieut.General - not present

Lieut.Colonel
Sir Robert Rich Bt.	24 Jun 1744*

* Wounded at Culloden

Major
John Wilson	17 Apr 1743

Captains
Richard Coren	3 Mar 1736	Lord Robert Kerr	21 Apr 1743*
James Thorne	21 Apr 1743	John Tucker	13 Jun 1744
John Romer	18 Jun 1744**	James Wolfe	23 Jun 1744***
William McKnight	25 Jun 1744	Thomas Hardy	26 Jun 1744
Peregrine Wentworth	17 Aug 1744		

* Killed at Culloden
** Wounded at Culloden
*** Brevet Major - Hawley's staff

Capt. Lieutenant
John Pett	10 Jun 1745

Lieutenants
John Felton	14 Apr 1740*	James Edmonds	15 Nov 1740**
William Neilson	25 Jan 1741	Thomas Schaak	26 Jan 1741
Joseph Higginson	25 Apr 1741***	Thomas Cooke	25 Jun 1744
John Gibson	25 Jun 1744	Joseph Partridge	17 Aug 1744
Jonas Thompson	17 Aug 1744	Thomas Brereton	10 Jun 1745
Martin Stapleton	10 Jun 1745	*Vacant*	

*Adjutant 27 Jan 1744
** Wounded at Culloden
*** Quartermaster 2 Nov 1737

Barrell's 4th Regiment - The Cloathing Book 1742
(Private collection.)

Ensigns

Thomas Hillary	30 Jan 1741	Michael Balfour	1 Mar 1741
Alexander Gordon	13 Jun 1744	John Brown	24 Jun 1744*
James Campbell	25 Jun 1744*	Jewett Cowart	25 Jun 1744
Richard Legge	17 Aug 1744	Charles LeGrys	21 Nov 1744
Cholmondley Brereton	1 May 1745	John Charlton	1 Aug 1745
William Dalmahoy	24 Aug 1745		

* Wounded at Culloden

Surgeon	John McIntosh	24 Feb 1745
Chaplain	John Duncan	2 May 1745

According to the morning state Barrell's paraded 2 field officers, 5 captains, 13 subalterns, 18 sergeants, 10 drummers and 325 rank and file. The Guildhall list on the other hand quotes 20 sergeants, 23 corporals, 10 drummers and 365 privates.

Losses were heavy, totalling 17 officers and men killed and 108 wounded. Moreover, only 29 out of the 103 rank and file returned as wounded survived to be awarded pensions:

Corporal John Adams, aged 34, lost the use of his right hand
Corporal John Griffith, aged 32, lost the use of his left leg
William Alexander, "wounded at Culloden"
Thomas Appleton, aged 25, lost the use of his left arm
David Bairnsfather, aged 40, wounded in the right leg
Peter Burford, aged 35, disabled in his left hand
James Butler, aged 22, lost his left arm
Matthew Chappington, aged 38, lost the use of his right arm
Simon Crocker, aged 27, lost the use of his right hand
John Dills, aged 55, "unfit for service by wounds received at Culloden"
David Drenan, aged 45, disabled in the right thigh
John Fawcett, aged 40, "wounded at Culloden"
Thomas Harris, wounded in the left leg
John Hobbs, "wounded at Culloden"
Samuel Hunt, agricultural labourer from Leicestershire, wounded in the head and right hand
Ralph Jackson, aged 24 from Oldham, disabled in his left hand
John Jenkins, aged 26, lost the use of his left arm
Thomas Kelly, aged 28, lost the use of his left leg
Thomas Knight, aged 44, disabled in the right leg
John Lee, aged 48, lost his right arm
David Lotty, aged 47, shot through the right arm
John Low, aged 32, a baker from Alford (Lincolnshire?), shot through the left leg and thigh
John Messenger, aged 52, "wounded at Culloden"
Isaac Midgely, aged 37 from Halifax, "Disabled in the left hand at Culloden besides 14 more wounds."
Thomas Pritchard, "wounded at Culloden"
Jonathan Scoon, aged 34, wounded in the head
John Telford, aged 39 from Dumfries, "wounded at Culloden"
John Tinlims, aged 30, disabled in his right hand and shoulder
George Webb, aged 52, shot through the left arm

Captain James Wolfe

They were attacked by the Camerons (the bravest clan amongst them), and 'twas for some time a dispute between the swords and bayonets; but the latter was found by far the most destructible weapon. The Regiment behaved with uncommon resolution, killing, some say, almost their own number, whereas forty of them were only wounded, and those not mortally and not above ten killed. They were, however, surrounded with superiority, and would have been all destroyed had not Col. Martin with his regiment (the left of the 2nd line of Foot) moved forward to their assistance, prevented mischief, and by a well-timed fire destroyed a great number of them and obliged them to run off.

Anonymous officer, Inverness 17 April 1746:[6]

Yesterday at One o Clock the Rebels began to cannonade us. We soon return'd their Salute with much better Success which they perceiving, gave over, and advanc'd briskly towards us Sword in Hand; but the Reception they met with soon convinced them of their Error. These that attacked were their best men, viz. the Camerons, MacDonalds and Stuarts of Appin. As our Regiment was on the Left of the Front, it fell to our share to bear the Brunt of the Attack; which to our Glory we did in a most Gallant Manner. Hardly a man in the Regiment but laid his Adversary at his Foot. I speak within Compass for several doubled their Number. The Loss of our Regiment is greater than any other. The Duke was in the Heat of the Action the whole Time, encouraging his Men, and I do assure you, took great Notice of our Behaviour, of which he was pleas'd to express his Pleasure.

P.S. I have just been on the Field of Battle, where lay 1500 of the Flower of the Highland Clans, besides those killed by the Horse in their Flight, which was no small Number.

Monro's 37th Regiment

Facing colour: Yellow (with Orange tinge), with gold lace for officers. The actual appearance of the uniform worn at Culloden is uncertain. Yellow lapels and linings are shown in the 1742 Cloathing Book, but the cuffs are red, edged with yellow lace. By 1748 however the uniform was much more conventional appearance with yellow cuffs and with white lace edged with red and blue zig-zags, and two yellow lines running down the middle. Button-hole loops were square ended.

Strictly speaking this regiment was Colonel Dejean's, in succession to Monro, killed at Falkirk, but most accounts of the battle still refer to the regiment as Monro's.

Colonel

Sir Robert Monro Bt	*17 Jun 1745**	Louis Dejean	9 Apr 1746

* Killed at Falkirk 17 Feb 1746

Lieut.Colonel

James Biggar	*27 Feb 1742*	William Deane	17 Feb 1746

* Killed at Falkirk 17 Feb 1746

Major

Solomon Blosset	19 Apr 1743

Monro's 37th Regiment - The Cloathing Book 1742
(Private collection.)

Captains

Thomas Timpson	7 Dec 1734	William Gee	28 Oct 1737
Thomas Buck	15 Jan 1740	James Adolphus D. Oughton	13 May 1742
Henry Wetherall	*4 Oct 1743**	*Samuel Hall*	*25 Jun 1744**
George Fitzgerald	26 Jun 1744	Samuel Boucher	7 May 1745**
James Kinneer	8 Aug 1745***	John Doyne	17 Feb 1746
Jordan Wren	17 Feb 1746		

* Killed at Falkirk 17 Feb 1746
** Adjutant 4 Jun 1742
*** Wounded at Culloden

Capt. Lieutenant

Thomas Goddard	17 Feb 1746

Lieutenants

Francis Jones	4 Nov 1740	Charles Fleury	4 Jun 1742
Loftus Cliffe	17 Jul 1742	Marshall Davies	25 Jun 1744
Apsley Newton	25 Jun 1744	Henry Graeme	26 Jun 1744
George Lort	7 May 1745*	Joseph Maddocks	11 Jul 1745
St.George Dalley	22 Jul 1745	John King	8 Aug 1745*
Robert Clayton Bayley	16 Jan 1746	Robert Clements	17 Feb 1746

* Wounded at Culloden

Ensigns

William Murdoch	25 Jun 1744*	John Dalley	6 May 1745**
George Brereton	5 May 1745	Maurice Cane	8 Aug 1745
Thomas Buck	12 Sep 1745	Arthur Obins	25 Sep 1745
Robert Harrison	16 Jan 1746	Felix Buckley	17 Feb 1746

* Wounded at Culloden
** Died of wounds 17 April 1746

Quartermaster	Henry Loftus	25 Apr 1742
Surgeon	*John Boucher*	*20 Jun 1727**
	John Douglas	31 Mar 1746
Chaplain	James Moore	18 Jun 1742

* Killed at Falkirk 17 Feb 1746

The morning state gives a strength of 2 field officers, 6 captains, 15 subalterns, 23 sergeants, 19 drummers and 426 rank and file, making it the strongest regiment on the field. The Guildhall figures cite the same 23 sergeants and 19 drummers, but add 24 corporals and quote a figure of 474 privates.

Casualties were very heavy, with 14 men killed on the spot and 68 wounded. Although this represents 43 fewer casualties than the 17 killed and 108 wounded reported by Barrell's, all of Monro's casualties were disproportionately concentrated on the grenadiers and the left flank companies of the regiment. Once again there was a heavy mortality rate amongst those initially returned as wounded and only 19 of the 68 wounded survived to claim a pension:

William Ashmore, aged 21, disabled in the left hand and shoulder

Arthur Buchan, aged 29, disabled in the right thigh

Luke Cunningham, a blacksmith from Limerick, shot through the body

John Davidson, disabled in the left hand and shoulder

John Dolloway, aged 27, disabled in the left thigh

Robert Farrington, aged 35, disabled in the left leg

William Gill, shot through the right elbow

Thomas Grant, disabled in both thighs

Isaac Gregg, aged 43, "disabled by fall at Culloden"

Thomas Griffith, aged 40, shot in the left knee

John Guest, disabled in the right arm

John Hawson, aged 39, shot in the left knee

William Irwin, aged 32, lost use of left leg

Thomas Lowns, aged 27, disabled in the left leg

Charles McLeland, shot through the right ankle

Edward McMullen of Dublin, "disabled in several parts of his body at Culloden"

Richard Moulton, aged 47, "disabled by a shot in his right leg"

John Perry, aged 23, disabled in the right leg

John Tovey, 55 years old, "born in the army", jaw shot away.

Lieutenant Loftus Cliffe to friend 17 April 1746[7]

"The Hurry I am in going to collect the number of killed and wounded, scarce allows me time to tell you, that Yesterday we had the bloodiest Battle with the Rebels that ever was in the Memory of Man. The same Morning we march'd from Nairn, and met the Gentry about Noon near Culloden, the Lord President's House, three miles from hence, where we cannonaded each other for some Time; at last the Rebels advanc'd against the Left of our Line where was Barrel's Regiment, and the late Sir Robert Monro's, now Col.De Jean's. Barrel's behaved very well, but was obliged to give Way to their Torrent that bore down upon them; Their whole force then fell upon the Left of ours where I had the Honour to command the Grenadier platoon; our Lads fought more like Devils than Men. In short we laid (to the best of my Judgement) about 1600 dead on the Spot and finished the Affair without the Help of any other Regiment. You may judge of the Work, for I had 18 men killed and wounded in my Platoon. I thank God I escaped free, but my Coat had six balls thro' it. I must now tell you, that in the Midst of the Action the Officer that led on the Camerons call'd to me to take Quarters; which I refus'd, and bid the Rebel Scoundrel advance, he did, and fir'd at me; but providentially miss'd his Mark: I then shot him dead, and took his Pistol and Dirk, which are extreamly neat.

The French have all surrendered Prisoners of war: We have taken their Cannon and Baggage; Lords Kilmarnock and Cromarty are among the Prisoners of Distinction.[8] Our Regiment had ample Revenge for the Loss of our late Colonel, Sir Robert, and the rest of our Officers, whom the Scoundrels murdered in cold blood, but (as I told Lord Kilmarnock) we had ample Revenge in hors. For I can with great Truth asure you, not one that attack'd us escaped alive, for we gave no Quarters nor would accept of any. Our Regiment took three Stand of colours. Our Wounded are Capt. Kinnier and Lieuts. Lort and King, and Ensign Dally kill'd. I now give you Joy of the Day; and be assur'd never was a more compleate Victory gained - Our Goals are full of them and they are brought in by Hundreds.

Anonymous corporal:[9]

On the 16th instant in the Forenoon, when we came within 300 yards of the Rebels they began to play their Cannon very briskly upon us; but as soon as we saw them pointed, we stoop'd down, and the Balls flew over our Heads. Two Pieces of our Cannon play'd from our Left to their Right, which kill'd many of them, and made their whole body determine to come down upon our Left, compos'd of Barrel's, Monro's and the Scots Fusiliers. When we saw them coming towards us in great Haste and Fury, we fired at about 50 Yards Distance, which made hundreds Fall; notwithstanding which, they were so numerous, that they still advanced, and were almost upon us before we had loaden again. We immediately gave them another full fire, the Front Rank charged their Bayonets Breast high, and the Center and Rear ranks kept a continual Firing, which in half an Hour's Time, routed their whole Army. Only Barrel's Regiment and ours was engaged, the Rebels designing to break or flank us; but our fire was so hot, most of us having discharged nine Shot each, that they were disappointed. The Loss of the Rebels in killed and wounded, is computed at 4500, and 2000 Prisoners, besides Numbers coming in every Day. Fitz James's Horse, with their Officers at the Head of them, surrender'd this Morning.

Campbell's 21st (Royal Scots Fusiliers) Regiment

Facing colour: Blue, with white lace bearing a blue zig-zag and a yellow line in 1742 and a black scroll in place of the zig-zag by 1748. Loops on buttonholes were square ended and the lace of the sleeves arranged in a ladder pattern. As a fusilier regiment the men belonging to the battalion companies were officially to wear grenadier style caps. Those worn in 1742 had a blue front bearing a white star of St.Andrew, superimposed in the centre of which was a green thistle on a red roundel enclosed by a yellow collar. Instead of the usual white horse of St. George displayed on the frontlet or small flap, there was a thistle depicted in its natural colours and the title *Royal Fuziliers*[10] around the edge. Officers' lace is uncertain. Ordinarily they should have had gold lace but a portrait from 1751 shows silver.

Colonel
John Campbell	1 Nov 1738	Major General 24 Feb 1744

Lieut.Colonel
Sir Andrew Agnew Bt.	2 Nov 1739	Governor of Blair Castle

Major
Hon. Charles Colvill	22 Feb 1741

Captains
John Crosbie	25 Mar 1724	Hon. William Leslie	16 Jan 1737
Thomas Oliphant	1 Sep 1739	Hon. Andrew Sandilands	14 Jul 1743
Norton Knatchbull	23 Jun 1744	George Monck	25 Jun 1744
Sir James Carnegie Bt.	26 Jun 1744	John Noble	1 May 1745
David Watson	21 May 1745		

* Governor of Aberdeen[11]
** Brevet Major 20 Mar 1742
*** Brevet Lieut. Col. 18 Jan 1746

Capt. Lieutenant
John Campbell Edmonstone   1 May 1745

Lieutenants

Edward Maxwell Browne	30 Mar 1742	Robert Buchannan	9 Jul 1742
Wynne Johnson	14 Jul 1743	Adam Livingston	26 Aug 1743
George Anderson	4 Jun 1744	Sir James Sharp Bt.	23 Jun 1744
Hon. John Colvill	25 Jun 1744	John Dalrymple	25 Jun 1744
James Chisholme[12]	25 Oct 1744	James Bellenden	1 May 1745
Hon. Charles Colvill	1 May 1745	Robert McGachan	1 May 1745

* Adjutant 25 Sep 1745

Second Lieutenants

John Chisholme	4 Jun 1744	James Pringle	8 Jun 1744
William Bellenden	23 Jun 1744	James, Lord Boyd[13]	25 Jun 1744
Archibald Campbell	25 Jun 1744	John Napier	1 May 1745
John Lindsay	1 May 1745	Duncan Campbell	1 May 1745
John Hay	1 Jul 1745	David Hope	1 Sep 1745
Middleton Grainge	10 Oct 1745		

Quartermaster	John Gillan	11 Jul 1745
Surgeon	Alexander Tough	10 Aug 1745
Chaplain	Charles Townsend	8 Jul 1742

Only one field officer (Major Charles Colvill) was present at Culloden according to the morning state, together with 5 captains, 13 subalterns, 21 sergeants, 14 drummers and 358 rank and file. Remarkably the Guildhall figures for once appear to be lower, evidencing 22 sergeants, 22 corporals, 12 drummers and only 336 privates. It should be noted however that at least one company was doing garrison duty at Blair Castle and another was at Aberdeen.

Seven men were returned as wounded, although only one of them, Mark Whitehead, wounded in the right thigh appeared before the board at Chelsea.

Private Edward Linn:
We waded to the knees in mud and dirt through the moor several times that day with a good will to be att them, and no wonder considering the fatigues we have undergone this winter by hunger and cold and marching day and night after them... Their spirited advance lasted but a short time with any kind of warmth, and they shifted away to our left. They came up very boldly & very fast all in a Cloud together, Sword in hand; they fired their pieces & flung them away, but we gave them so Warm a Reception that we kept a Continuall Closs ffireing upon them with our Small Arms; besides, 2 or 3 of our Cannon gave them a Closs with grape shott which galled them very much...They thought it was such a bad day that our firelocks would not fire, but scarce one in our regiment missed firing, but kept them dry with our coat laps... I never saw a field thicker of dead.

FOURTH BRIGADE

Wolfe's 8th Regiment

Facing colour: Blue, although the 1742 *Cloathing Book* erroneously shows yellow - an error repeated by Millan's *Army List*. In 1748 Morier depicted white lace with a yellow zig-zag, and pointed end loops at the button holes, arranged in ladder pattern on the sleeves. Officers had gold lace. Grenadier caps had a white horse on a red roundel enclosed within the garter.

Again one of the smaller units on the field, Wolfe's had suffered quite badly at Falkirk in January, where five captains alone were killed besides those wounded.

Colonel
Edward Wolfe	25 Apr 1745	Major General - not present

Lieut.Colonel
Edward Martin	1 May 1745

Major
John LaFausille[14]	17 Feb 1746	vice Grey promoted to 14th Foot
		Brevet Maj 15 June 43

Captains
John Dallons	*31 Aug 1733★*	*Peter Guerin*	*20 Jun 1739★*
Thomas Lauder	*12 Jan 1740★*	*William Hele*	*7 Feb 1741★*
Malcolm Hamilton	*15 Jun 1743★*	Arthur Loftus	4 Oct 1743
Philip Jennings	26 Jun 1744	John Ekins	29 Nov 1745
William Catherwood	17 Feb 1746	John Cook	17 Feb 1746
Charles Desclousseaux	17 Feb 1746	Nehemiah Donellan	17 Feb 1746
Henry Rogers	17 Feb 1746	Richard Meggott	17 Feb 1746

★ killed at Falkirk 17 Jan 1746

Capt. Lieutenant
Thomas Ashe Lee	17 Feb 1746	From 59th Foot

Lieutenants
Richard Knight	13 May 1742	Thomas Thompson	15 Jun 1743
William Rickson	14 Jul 1743	Jacob Conway	24 Sep 1743
Joseph Artieres	25 Jun 1744	Francis Wilkinson	25 Jun 1744
Thomas Paske	15 Oct 1744	Charles Hemington	29 Nov 1745
John Beckwith	17 Feb 1746	John Caillaud	17 Feb 1746
John Corrance	17 Feb 1746	John Trollope	17 Feb 1746

Ensigns
Thomas Troughear	20 Apr 1744	William Wright	20 Apr 1744
Calthorpe Harrington	25 Jun 1744	Thomas Spencer Wilson	25 Jun 1744
Henry Rogers	10 Oct 1744	James Webb	15 Oct 1744
Robert Berry	17 Feb 1746	John Ellis	17 Feb 1746
James Davison	17 Feb 1746	Robert Bruce	17 Feb 1746★

★ Wounded at Culloden

Adjutant	Paul Pigou	11 Dec 1735
Quartermaster	Joseph Walworth	24 Feb 1746
Surgeon	Robert Miller	13 Sep 1745
Chaplain	Arthur Young	16 Dec 1739

According to the morning state there was 1 field officer (Lieutenant Colonel Edward Martin), 7 captains, 14 subalterns, 17 sergeants, 11 drummers and 324 rank and file present. The Guildhall list gives 19 sergeants, 22 corporals, 18 drummers and 387 privates.

Ensign Robert Bruce, commissioned just two months before the battle, was the only recorded casualty.

Captain-Lieutenant Thomas Ashe Lee:[15]

Poor Barrell's regiment were sorely pressed by those desperadoes and outflanked. One stand of their colours was taken; Collonel Riches hand cutt off in their defence... We marched up to the enemy, and our left, outflanking them, wheeled in upon them; the whole then gave them 5 or 6 fires with vast execution, while their front had nothing left to oppose us, but their pistols and broadswords; and fire from their center and rear (as, by this time, they were 20 or 30 deep) was vastly more fatal to themselves, than us. It was surprising they stood so long at such disadvantage.

Anonymous correspondent 18 April[16]

Barrel's Regiment was hard wrought by the Rebels, who pushed all their strength against them, and took two Pieces of Cannon from them; but our Regiment being ordered to flank the Rebels, we soon made the Place too hot for them, retook the Cannon, and took a great Number of Prisoners; more than we should have done, had we known of their Orders, which, was, spare neither Man, Woman, nor Child.

Ligonier's 59th Regiment

Facing colour: Buff, with gold lace for officers. Regiment was raised after the publication of the1742 *Cloathing Book*, so the earliest illustration is the 1748 one by Morier, which shows white lace with a yellow stripe set between a green stripe and scroll. The button-hole loops were square-ended.

Strictly speaking this regiment was Harry Conway's, in succession to Ligonier, who had died of pleurisy shortly after the battle of Falkirk in January, but like the 37th Foot was still being referred to by the name of its former colonel. Following the disbandment of the original 42nd Regiment (Oglethorpe's) and ten regiments of Army-controlled Marines which had ranked as the 44th to 49th Foot, this regiment was re-designated as the 48th Regiment in 1748.

Colonel
Hon. Henry Seymour Conway   6 Apr 1746

Lieut.Colonel
George Stanhope   10 Apr 1743

Major
John Morrice   2 Feb 1741

Captains

David Douglas	23 Jan 1741	William Sparke	24 Jan 1741*
Benjamin Price	5 Aug 1742	Stuart Douglas	23 Jul 1743
Doyley Bromfield	17 Mar 1744	James Mercer	25 Jun 1744
William Marshall	26 Jun 1744	Robert Dobson	19 Aug 1745
Roger Morris	13 Sep 1745		

* Wounded at Culloden

Capt.Lieutenant

Amy Peter Piaget	19 Aug 1745

Lieutenants

William Oman	21 Jan 1741	Hugh Grant	22 Jan 1741
Charles Ramsay	24 Jan 1741	George Douglas	27 Jan 1741
William Morris	4 Jun 1742	Thomas Dyson	25 Jun 1744
Somerville McQueen	25 Jun 1744	John Gordon	22 Nov 1744
Richard Bowyer	11 Apr 1745	Richard Lloyd	12 May 1745
Hercules Ellis	24 Sep 1745	Henry Brierly	17 Feb 1746

Ensigns

Waterhouse Crymble	25 Jun 1744	Theodore Barbutt	22 Nov 1744
John Walsham	4 Apr 1745	John Frazer	24 Apr 1745*[17]
William Brereton	12 May 1745	Thomas Thornley	19 Aug 1745
Isaac Remple	24 Sep 1745**	Thomas Daniel	15 Oct 1745
Maurice White	15 Oct 1745	( ) Studdard	17 Feb 1746
James McDonald	17 Feb 1746	George Neale	16 Apr 1746***

* Probably not present
** Adjutant 22 Mar 1744
*** Probably not present

Quartermaster	Thomas Lovett	27 Jan 1744
Surgeon	Samuel Palmer	17 Jan 1741
Chaplain	Henry Tilson	17 Jan 1741

At Culloden it mustered all 3 field officers, 5 captains, 16 subalterns, 21 sergeants, 16 drummers and 325 rank and file according to the morning state, and a very similar 21 sergeants, 22 corporals, 16 drummers and 342 privates in the Guildhall list. One man was returned as killed and 5 wounded, including: William Knight, described as disabled in his right foot when he appeared before the Chelsea board.

Sempill's 25th (Edinburgh) Regiment

Facing colour: Yellow, with gold lace for officers. Other ranks had white lace with a red and blue zig-zag in 1742, but this had changed to a blue/yellow/black edging on both sides by 1748. Pointed ended loops in 1742 were likewise changed for square ended ones, but the sleeve lace was arranged in a ladder pattern throughout.

Colonel

Hugh, Lord Sempill[18]	25 Apr 1745

Lieut.Colonel

Sir David Cunynghame Bt.	25 Feb 1746

Sempill's 25th (Edinburgh) Regiment
Victorian reworking of an image in The Cloathing Book 1742
(Private collection.)

Major
Richard Worge	25 Feb 1746

Captains
James Dalrymple	5 Mar 1723	George Scott	7 May 1742
Henry St.Clair	7 May 1742	William Lucas	28 Sep 1743
Thomas Lowrie	25 Jun 1744	Charles Leslie	8 May 1745
James L. Campbell	25 May 1745*	Hon. Bluet Wallop	25 May 1745
James Hamilton	25 Feb 1746		

* (of Ardkinglas) Grenadier Company

Capt. Lieutenant
Hon. David Home	25 Feb 1746

Lieutenants
Charles Stephens	1 Jun 1739	Archibald Campbell	13 Mar 1741
Thomas Goodricke	8 May 1742	Patrick Lundin	9 May 1742
Walter Brodie	28 Sep 1743	Archibald Douglas	25 Jun 1744
James Manwaring	25 Jun 1744	Sir Guy Carleton	1 May 1745
Adam Cockburne	25 May 1745*	Robert Knight	29 May 1745
John Stothard	17 Feb 1746	Francis Gore	25 Feb 1746

* Adjutant

Ensigns
Lewis Jones	25 May 1742	Edward Randall	26 May 1742
Robert Melville	26 Mar 1744	Robert Orrock	25 Jun 1744
Robert Watson	25 Jun 1744	John Campbell	1 May 1745
Alexander Symmer	25 May 1745	Charles Gilman	29 May 1745*
James Stratton	1 Sep 1745	Alexander Campbell	17 Feb 1746
William Henson	25 Feb 1746		

* Quartermaster   31 Mar 1743

Surgeon	George Monro	6 Jun 1744
Chaplain	Anthony Chester	11 Aug 1737

The morning state reveals this was one of the strongest regiments on the field with all three field officers present (albeit Lord Sempill, was actually a brigade commander), together with 5 captains, 15 subalterns, 20 sergeants, 14 drummers and 420 rank and file. The Guildhall figures are also high, quoting 20 sergeants, 25 corporals, 19 drummers and 487 privates.

> One man was killed and 13 wounded, but only 3 lived to claim pensions:
> Thomas Hoskin, wounded in his right thigh
> John Lemmon, disabled in his left arm
> John McDonald, "unfit by reason of a bruise at Culloden"

There are no known narratives from members of this regiment, which took part in Huske's counter-attack. The grenadier company, commanded by Campbell of Ardkinglas afterwards took formal possession of Inverness. A fairly lengthy (and much quoted) account of atrocities committed after the battle purporting to have been obtained from the Quartermaster is contained in Forbes' *Lyon in Mourning*[19] however considerable doubt has to be cast on the truth of his story since he is identified as a Lachlan Shaw. In fact the Quartermaster was actually Ensign Charles Gillman.

Grenadier, 13th Foot 1753, after Lieutenant William Baillie. Although dating from some years after the battle this figure provides a pretty good idea of the typical appearance of a grenadier at Culloden. (S Reid)

NB: Two of the reserve regiments were effectively assigned to other brigades at the start of the battle; Pulteney's 13th to the First Brigade, and Ligonier's 59th to the Third Brigade.

Pulteney's 13th Regiment

Facing colour: Philemot (brownish yellow), with silver lace for officers. Other ranks had white lace with a yellow zig-zag and no button-loops on the lapels in 1742, but by 1748 this had changed to a double zig-zag line (one yellow, one blue), with pointed ended loops on the lapels. At both dates the lace on the sleeves was arranged in ladder pattern.

As will be seen from the list below this was another regiment with a higher than usual proportion of Scots officers - a trend that continued for many years afterwards.

Colonel
Harry Pulteney	5 Jul 1737	Major General - not present

Lieut.Colonel
Thomas Cockayne	9 Sep 1744	Brevet Lt.Col. 29 May 1744

Major
Christopher Legard	9 Sep 1744

Captains
Robert Bullman	20 Jan 1736	Hon. John Craufurd	20 Apr 1743*
Thomas Lyster	11 Aug 1743	John Stafford	25 Jun 1744
David Chapeau	26 Jun 1744	George Mackenzie	9 Sep 1744
Noel Furye	22 Nov 1744	Daniel Nicholas	1 May 1745
Donald Clark	29 May 1745		

* Brevet Major 6 Jun 1745

Capt. Lieutenant
William Jones	1 May 1745

Lieutenants
John Hadzor	1 Feb 1727*	Richard Hargrave	24 Jan 1741
David Duvernet	25 Apr 1741	Patrick Lyon	25 Apr 1741
Sir David Lyndsay Bt.	17 Mar 1744	Sackville Fox	25 Jun 1744
Joseph Harrison	25 Jun 1744	John Royden Hughes	9 Sep 1744
David Ogilvy	13 Nov 1744	Samuel Edhouse	22 Feb 1745
Daniel Daniel	23 Feb 1745**	Robert Hilton	1 May 1745

* Surgeon
** Adjutant 20 Apr 1743

Ensigns
Honywood Haddock	17 Sep 1743	John Skottowe	17 Sep 1743
James Selleck	20 May 1744	William Baillie	25 Jun 1744
John Pinhorne	25 Jun 1744	Abraham Clarke	13 Nov 1744

Corporal Jones, 13th Foot 1753, after Lieutenant William Baillie. (S Reid)

Robert Cholmley	22 Feb 1745	Isaac Yestes	23 Feb 1745
George Holliday	1 May 1745	John Naylour	7 Jun 1745
James Garnham	17 Feb 1746		

Chaplain	Alexander Colquhoun	24 Aug 1745

The morning state lists 2 field officers, 6 captains, 14 subalterns, 23 sergeants, 19 drummers and 410 rank and file present, while the Guildhall figures are; 23 sergeants, 26 corporals, 18 drummers and 479 privates.

No casualties were recorded.

Batereau's 62nd Regiment

Facing colour: Yellow. No real information is available since the regiment was raised after the publication of the 1742 Cloathing Book and was then disbanded at the end of the war in 1748, before Morier could paint it. However Millan's Army List notes yellow facings.

This unit should not of course be confused with the later 62nd Regiment formed in 1756.

Colonel
John Batereau	29 Mar 1742

Lieut.Colonel
Robert Catherwood	31 Mar 1742

Major
Richmond Webb	17 Feb 1746[20]	vice Charles Jeffreys promoted into 34th.

Captains
Anthony Jephson	25 Apr 1742	William Supple	25 Apr 1742
Nicholas Price	27 Apr 1742	Stratford Eyre	14 May 1742
David Urquhart	8 Jul 1742	Hon. Thomas Gage	1 Jan 1743
Thomas Carter	20 Apr 1743		

Capt.Lieutenant
George Maxwell	1 Jan 1743

Lieutenants
Robert Stronge	29 Apr 1742	Thomas Stone	1 May 1742
Richard Gresham	3 May 1742	Lewis Thomas	5 May 1742
Francis Manning	6 May 1742	Jocelyn White	1 May 1744
William Cooper	2 May 1744	John Debutts	27 Dec 1744
Robert Jephson	29 Dec 1744	John Hansard	9 Jul 1745
Robert Creighton	17 Feb 1746*		

* vice Thomas Ashe Lee promoted into 8th.

2nd Lieutenants
William Playstowe	15 May 1742	Alexander Conyngham	1 Jan 1743
Thomas Backhouse	1 May 1744	John Galland	2 May 1744*

James Gage	3 May 1744	Francis Alesieu	27 Dec 1744**
Edward Vernon	29 Dec 1744	John Lloyd	6 Feb 1745
William Moore	9 Jul 1745		

* Quartermaster 23 Oct 1745
** Adjutant

Ensigns

Thomas Mitchell	26 May 1742	Edward Johnston	2 May 1744
Caleb Wood	3 May 1744	Jasper Desbrisay	27 Dec 1744
Allan Jeffries	29 Dec 1744	John Ward	1 Jun 1745
Edmund Turner	9 Jul 1745	Henry French	7 Sep 1745
John Laulhe	26 Sep 1745		

Surgeon	Joshua Pilot	1 May 1742
Chaplain	Michael Broughton	29 Mar 1742

The morning state gives 1 field officer, 7 captains, 19 subalterns, 24 sergeants, 18 drummers and 354 rank and file present at Culloden, while the Guildhall list also evidences 24 sergeants and 18 drummers, but adds 33 corporals and gives the number of privates as 384.

The regiment reported just 3 wounded: Captain Thomas Carter; and Privates William Matthews, wounded in his right side, and Daniel McIntosh, who lost his left leg

Blakeney's 27th (Inniskilling) Regiment

Facing colour: Buff, with silver lace for officers. Other ranks had white lace with twin wavy yellow lines in 1742, but no button loops and no lace on the sleeves. This was probably added in 1743 by the white lace with a yellow stripe between black and blue zig-zags as depicted by Morier in 1748. Morier also shows pointed loops and the common ladder pattern on the sleeves. Grenadier caps had a blue roundel bearing a three turreted castle, with Inniskilling above.

Colonel

William Blakeney	27 Jun 1737	Maj.General - Governor of Stirling

Lieut.Colonel

Francis Leighton	6 Jul 1737

Major

John Chambre	12 Sep 1742

Captains

Edward Todd	12 Jan 1740*	Richard Kellett	10 Mar 1742*
William Grenfield	27 Apr 1742	William Haviland	7 Sep 1742
Alexander Dunlop	24 Sep 1742	Archibald Gordon	14 Oct 1742
John Dalrymple	8 Jun 1744*	George A. Blakeney	17 Feb 1746**
James Sandilands	17 Feb 1746	John Goodenough	17 Feb 1746

* Killed at Falkirk 17 Jan 1746
** Quartermaster 27 Apr 1742

Blakeney's 27th (Inniskilling) Regiment -
Victorian reworking of an image in The Cloathing Book 1742
(Private collection.)

Capt. Lieutenant

William Edmondstoun	8 Jun 1744	Killed at Falkirk 17 Jan 1746
Eyre Massey		17 Feb 1746

Lieutenants

Robert Creed	27 Apr 1742*	William Fowler	4 Jul 1742
Charles Tucker	4 Jul 1742	Cuppage Fairfield	24 Sep 1742
Mark Weeks	1 Oct 1742	James Holmes (1)	8 Jun 1744
James Holmes (2)	17 Feb 1746	James Hawley	25 Feb 1746
Gabriel Christie	25 Feb 1746	John Hancock	14 Mar 1746

* Adjutant 10 Mar 1742

** Killed at Falkirk 17 Jan 1746

Ensigns

Thomas Hepworth	25 Aug 1742	Hugh Fraser	24 Sep 1742
Robert Elliot	1 Oct 1742	James Parker	31 Aug 1744
John Blakeney	30 Jul 1745	Roger Jones	17 Feb 1746
Benjamin Vaughton	17 Feb 1746	Francis Caulfield	25 Feb 1746
John Kirkpatrick	25 Feb 1746		

Surgeon	George Eagle	4 Apr 1745
Chaplain	Charles Coote	14 Oct 1743

The morning state lists 2 field officers, 4 captains, 14 subalterns, 24 sergeants, 12 drummers and 300 rank and file, which is reasonably close to the Guildhall's 25 sergeants, 22 corporals, 12 drummers and 336 privates.

No casualties were reported.

UNBRIGADED

The Argyleshire Men

The fourth Scottish unit to fight at Culloden were the Highlanders, usually but not entirely accurately referred to as the Argyle Militia. It in fact comprised eight companies rather than the usual ten, or which only four belonged to the Argyle Militia. Of the others; three belonged to Loudoun's 64th Highlanders and the last to the 43rd Highlanders. Under the overall command of Lieutenant Colonel John Campbell of the 64th Highlanders it was divided into two small battalions or wings during the battle, each comprising two companies of regulars and two of militia. One battalion was assigned to help guard the baggage train, while the other served with some distinction in the Culwhiniac Enclosures on the left flank of the army. This unit, led by Captain Colin Campbell of Ballimore included his own company of the 64th Highlanders, one company (wrongly identified by Campbell of Airds as a militia unit) of the 43rd Highlanders under Captain Dugald Campbell of Auchrossan, together with Captain John Campbell of Achnaba's militia company and a second militia company, from Glenorchy, under Captain Duncan Campbell.

The battalion had no recognisable uniform. Campbell of Auchrossan no doubt wore scarlet regimentals with the buff facings of the 43rd, while the 64th officers had white facings. Whether their men were similarly dressed is questionable. Achrossan commanded an Additional Company made up of new recruits and the 64th had similarly been in the process of recruiting when the Rising began. All of them, regulars and militia alike, seem to have worn their ordinary Highland clothing, with red or yellow crosses in their bonnets. The significance of the two different colours is unclear but they may have served to distinguish between the men of the regular companies and the militia.

The "Argyleshire Men" are not accounted for in the morning state, but according to the Guildhall list there were 32 sergeants, 30 corporals, 9 drummers and 430 privates in total. In all 9 members of the 64th were killed and wounded, including Ballimore, who was killed and Dougal McPhail, disabled in the left shoulder and thigh. Only one member of the Argyle Militia was returned as a casualty; Captain John Campbell of Achnaba , who was mortally wounded.

Lieutenant Colonel John Campbell (64th) to father, Inverness 16 April 1746:[21]
"I have just time to inform you that we have gained a compleat victory over the rebels. The main body of my corps was ordered as a guard for the baggage, by which means I had no opportunity of seeing the affair distinctly & must therefore differ writing particularly till another opportunity. Part of our men were engaged & behaved incomparably well amongst whom Ballimore was killed and Achnaba dangerously wounded. I believe there were above a Thousand dead of the rebels on the field & five hundred prisoners. On our side about 40 men killed. No officer of note but Lord Robert Kerr."

Bligh's 20th Regiment
Victorian reworking of an image in The Cloathing Book 1742
(Private collection.)

Wolfe's 8th Regiment
Victorian reworking of an image in The Cloathing Book 1742
(Private collection.)

Royal Scotch Fuziliers - Victorian reworking of an image in The Cloathing Book 1742
(Private collection.)

10th Dragoons - Victorian reworking of an image in The Cloathing Book 1742
(Private collection.)

11th Dragoons - Victorian reworking of an image in The Cloathing Book 1742
(Private collection.)

Officer and sergeant of Highland Regiment after Van Gught. Although the Argyle Militia companies were far from regular, this is a pretty fair representation of clothing worn by the officers of the 43rd and 64th Highlanders at Culloden. The 43rd had buff facings at this time, while the 64th had white.

Grenadier cap worn by officer of 43rd Highlanders; although following the same broad design, the quality of the workmanship is far superior. (S Reid)

Campbell of Airds:[22]

"April 16th - A Glorious Day. The army decamped early, officers & soldiers in the Highest Spirits. Col. Campbell with his men & a party of the light Horse were sent before, to Examine the Roads and woods in the way. The army marched in four Columns, when within two miles of Culloden, the advanced party halted till the army came up & drew up in Battle order. The Duke having advice of the Enemie's being on a muir & rising ground above Culloden, march'd in Battle order up to the Height of the muir, that he might attack them in front & prevent them giving him the slip either to the right or left, & to keep the advantage of the Weather which favoured us as it blew full in their faces with smart showers.

The orders given Coll Campbell was to divide his men on the Right and Left wings of the army & so to march on till the Engagement begun, when they were to retire to Guard the Baggage. Capt. Campbell of Ballimore with his Company, the Glenurchay, Achnaba's and Dugald Campbell's Companys of militia were detached to the left, the Col. with the rest being on the Right.

In advancing the Duke made some short stops to ease his Troops at times marching them in platoons & in Battle order till near the Enemy, when he formed & brought up his Cannon.

The Dragoons & light horse were divided on the right & left took possession of a Battery on the Enemies left & made some prisoners before the battle begun.

The Rebels had three Batteries at a Cottage above the parks of Culloden, from which they begun to play on our Line about one in the afternoon. Their Complement was soon returned by our Cannon from the right Center & left. Theirs did little or no Execution but ours a great deal & disordered them so, that as they could not stand it, they Endeavoured to break in upon our Line Sword in hand & advanced very resolutely, but were received with such a Closs & hot fire from our Small Arms, that they soon gave ground & fled out right - which by the way was the pleasantest sight I ever beheld. In the pursuit the Dragoons & Light Horse made terrible slaughter of them.

The Cannonading Continued about nine minutes & the whole was over in less than an hour.

General Bland with the Cavalry Commanded on the left, when advancing to Flank the Enemies Right was stpt by two high Stone park Dykes that lay in his way, & went down to the Water of Nairn, on which Ballimore & his command were ordered to break down them Dykes & make way for the Horse which they Executed & taking advantage of the second Dyke as a Breast Work fire Closs on a strong party of the Rebels that then formed the Right. Composed of Lord John Drummond's men being part of the Enemy's second line & putting them to Disorder, General Bland advanced with the Cavalry & cut numbers of them to pieces.

It was passing a slap in the second Dyke that Ballimore was Shot Dead, and that Achnaba received his wound of which he Dyed next day. The right of our army got little to do, the greatest pressure lighted on Barrell's Regiment who were once disordered, but being supported by Munroes & Sempill's Soon form'd, clos'd their Ranks & did great Execution. The Scots Fusiliers, who behaved gloriously made the first break amongst the Enemy without the loss on one man. They had the Duke's particular thanks. Saying it was owing to them the victory was so cheap. There never was a more Compleat Victory obtained. We got all the Enemies Cannon, ammunition, & a good part of their

Baggage. His R.H. acted not only the part of a Generall but aid de Camp, was all the time in the lines giving orders, with the same collness as a Judge sitting on his bench.

The Troops all behaved remarkably well, and what I believe is very singular, not a single man turn'd his back or come off from the Line. Even the few wounded men came off in Spirits.

Our loss was surprisingly small. The only officer of Distinction killed was Lord Robert Kerr & anbout 40 private men.

Of the Enemy at least 1500 fell in the field & Chase. Some say upwards of 2000 and that of their best men mostly Clans & numbers of Gentlemen.

There are many prisoners but as many more still bringing in, the Exact number cannot be ascertained."

1   This chapter (and the following one on the cavalry) could not have been written without the assistance of Dr. John Houlding, who generously interrogated his personal database of 18th century officers to provide a snapshot of all those belonging to the Culloden regiments on April 16, 1746.

2   Brevetted Lieutenant Colonel 16 April 1746 - which may be a battlefield promotion - and afterwards noted to be serving as Aide de Camp to Lieutenant General St.Clair.

3   Ordinarily Lockhart might have expected to succeed to the lieutenant colonelcy as of right, following Powell's death in action but he himself was taken prisoner at Falkirk and although he afterwards made his escape, Jeffreys was brought in from outside over his head.

4   "Extract of a Letter from a Sergeant of the Old Buffs, to his Friend in Newcastle, dated Inverness, April 18." *Newcastle Courant*

5   Or so it may be inferred from the fact that the 1 September return noted that he was recovering from his wounds in Edinburgh.

6   "Extract of a Letter from an Officer in Barrel's Regiment, dated at Inverness, April 17." *Newcastle Courant*

7   This account appeared in a number of contemporary newspapers. The text here is taken from *The Newcastle Journal*. The version in the *York Courant* apparently identifies the author as a Captain Clifton, but no officer of that name was serving with the 37th. Moreover the commander of the left flank grenadier platoon would have been a lieutenant, not a captain. Hence Lieutenant Lofthouse Cliffe appears to be the officer in question.

8   Cromartie had in fact been captured in an ambush near Dunrobin on the day before Culloden.

9   "Extract of a Letter from a Corporal in Monro's Regiment, dated Inverness, April 19. *Newcastle Journal*

10 This may be a copyists error, omitting the word *Scots*

11 A very old officer indeed, who had actually been a captain since 5 January 1707!

12 He and Ensign John Chisholm were elder brothers of Roderick Og Chisholm, who died leading their Jacobite clansmen at Culloden. John Prebble errs in stating they served with the 1st (Royal) regiment - the Royal scots.

13 The son of Lord Kilmarnock, a Jacobite officer taken prisoner at Culloden and afterwards executed.

14 Noted in late March to be bringing up a draft of 500 sick and reinforcements.

15 O'Callaghan, *History of the Irish Brigades in the Service of France*, 450.

16 "Extract of a Letter from Wolfe's Regiment at Inverness, April 18." *Newcastle Courant*

17 Exchanged with George Neale (q.v.) into 39th Foot 16 April 1746

18 Sempill is shown on plans of the battle as commanding the left of the front line, rather than the 4th Brigade to which his regiment belonged.

19 Forbes, *Lyon in Mourning* Vol.2:298

20 Vice Charles Jeffreys, promoted into 34th Foot

21 National Library of Scotland MS3735/278

22 National Library of Scotland MS3735/290

One of the famous "Mutineer" prints depicting a piper of the 43rd Highlanders in 1743. The significance of the device on the pipe banner is unknown. Coloured versions of the print show a red cross on a yellow ground

Cavalry Regiments

For some reason the cavalry are included in neither the morning state, nor the Guildhall list and it is therefore rather more difficult to establish just how many actually fought at Culloden.

Cobham's 10th Dragoons

Facing colour: Yellow, with silver lace for officers. Saddle housing in 1742 were yellow with an elaborate red and black embroidered edging and a device of a knight's helmet and trophies appearing on both saddle-cloth and flounced holster caps. In 1748 however Morier shows a much more modern style with a plain white/black/white edging, a red cartouche in the rear corner of the saddle-cloth bearing an X over D for 10th Dragoons, and a GR cipher on the unflounced holster caps.

Colonel

Richard, Viscount Cobham	1 Jun 1745	Field Marshal - not present

Lieut. Colonel

John Jordan	4 Feb 1741	wounded at Falkirk - not at Culloden

Major Peter Chaban 31 Aug 1744

Captains

George Buckley	25 Apr 1741	Charles Hamilton	14 Jul 1743
Edward Goddard	31 Aug 1744		

Capt. Lieutenant

Charles Draper	31 Aug 1744

Lieutenants

John Tempest	19 Mar 1741	Samuel Gowland	25 Apr 1741
Thomas Carver	14 Jul 1743	Robert Winde	1 Feb 1744
Edward Harvey	31 Aug 1744		

Cornets

David Bell	12 Aug 1741*	William Beckwith	31 Oct 1741
Samuel Carter	14 Jul 1743	William Augustus Pitt	1 Feb 1744
Robert Atkinson	31 Aug 1744	Michael Greenhough	30 Jul 1745
* Adjutant	21 Jan 1744		

Surgeon	Samuel Aubrey	17 Mar 1727
Chaplain	Horace Hammond	3 Feb 1742

According to a parade state dated 28 March 1746, two weeks before the battle the regiment had 276 men present and four months later on 1 September it mustered 287 troopers present (including 7 new recruits), one man sick and 13 "on command", besides officers and NCOs. As to the latter there were 18 sergeants and 10 drummers.

Two squadrons of Cobham's served on the left wing in support of Kerr's, and one on the right, which no doubt accounts for the regiment's light casualties.

As Trooper Bradshaw relates below, only one man was killed and none were wounded, but the regiment did lose four horses killed and five wounded.

Trooper(?) Enoch Bradshaw to brother, Stonehaven 11 May 1746:[1]

… Your news papers give you a tolerable account, so I shall not, nor can I, give you a better with the compass of a letter. Since the last I sent you we find kill'd amongst the rebels no less than ten colonels, seven majors, fifteen captains, and as to lieutenants and ensigns, a volume of them. I leave you guess at the number of rank and file that must fall. In short, 'tis mine and every bodie's opinion no history can brag of so singular a victory and so few of our men lost, that we lost but one man; tho' I fear I shall lose my horse, he having at this moment of writing a ball in his left buttock. 'Twas pretty near Enoch that time, but, thank God, a miss is as good as a mile, as we say in Gloustershire. And now we have the pleasure of a bed and not hard duty; but for six weeks before the battle few of Cobham's heroes (thank God that is our character from the Duke and the general officers, except General Hawley, who does not love us because our regiment spoke truth about Falkirk job), I say for six weeks before I had not my cloaths off once, and had it not been for our dear Bill, we had all been starved, only for the good loaves he order'd for the army, and some provisions that came by shipping...

Anonymous:[2]

At the Beginning our Glorious Duke came up to Cobham's Dragoons and clapping some of them on the shoulders, called out "One Brush, my lads for the Honour of old Cobham, upon which rather like Devils than men, they broke through the enemy's flank and a total Rout followed. The Dragoons and Light Horse pursued, calling Cut Hard, Pay 'em home etc.

Cavalry standards are very poorly recorded at this period. While this particular guidon is not believed to have been carried at Culloden it is typical of the style used by Dragoon regiments at the time. (S Reid)

Kerr's 11th Dragoons

Facing colour: Uncertain. 1742 *Cloathing Book* shows the white facings to be expected on a regiment originally raised in Scotland, and red breeches. Morier on the other hand shows buff facings, including the breeches - as confirmed in the 1751 Warrant. Silver lace for officers. Saddle housing styles as for Cobham's above.

Colonel

Lord Mark Kerr	29 May 1732	General - not present	

Lieut. Colonel

William, Earl of Ancrum	22 Jun 1745	Brevet Colonel	4 Jun 1745

Major

Mark Anthony Saurin	20 Nov 1745

Captains

Francis Bushell	31 May 1732	William Gardner	10 May 1742
William Robert Adair	20 Nov 1745		

Capt. Lieutenant

Alexander Stuart	20 Nov 1745

Lieutenants

George Whitmore	10 May 1742	Guildford Killigrew	7 Sep 1742
George Lawson Hall	31 Aug 1744	Simon Polhill	30 Jul 1745
Gabriel Bilston	20 Nov 1745		

Cornets

Thomas Bygrave	10 May 1742*	Salem Philby	8 Sep 1742
John Broughton	21 Apr 1743	John Throckmorton	31 Aug 1744
James Jenkinson	30 Jul 1745	Benjamin Barber	20 Nov 1745
* Adjutant	23 Oct 1745		

Surgeon	Andrew Craufurd	11 Dec 1735
Chaplain	Patrick St.Clair	22 Jul 1715

The 28 March parade state lists 276 soldiers present, including 18 sick, for a total of 294 men together with 283 horses. A further 26 sick men and 54 horses had been left behind. By 1 September some of the sick had returned for it was then reported to have 312 men fit and only 16 men sick in the charge of a Sergeant Green. In addition to Green there were a further 17 sergeants and 12 drummers.

All three squadrons served on the left wing in a brigade commanded by Humhrey Bland. The regiment led the assault over the re-entrant to the west of Culchunaig against some Jacobite infantry under Lord Ogilvy and Gordon of Avochie, which no doubt accounts for its relatively heavy casualties, especially in horses.

Three men were returned as killed at Culloden with a further three wounded, but four horses were also killed and no fewer than 15 wounded.

Captain-Lieutenant Alexander Stuart of Dunearn to brother, Culloden 17 April 1746:[3]
I have only time to tell you we have got a compleat Victory - for the particular details of the Action I refer you to Miss Willie. The battle was yesterday about one o'clock. 2000 of the Rebels killed - a great many prisoners taken since - for hardly any were taken in the action. Above 5000 stand of Arms, 7 pieces of Cannon, 8 colours, and all their ammunition and wagons. I received no hurt, though pretty nigh being demolisht. I wish you joy of such a glorious action - which has put an end to the Rebellion!

Same, 24 April 1746:
I have nothing to add to my letter to Miss Willie, but that I brought in with a party of Dragoons from near Corryburgh ten miles from Inverness up Wade's road, My Lord Balmerino, Major Glasgo, and 27 French officers and soldiers, all which French are already embarked and sailed for France. Ld Balmerino says there are not 20 Highlanders any where together. He surrendered himself, he, Perth, Tullibardine, and Lord Ogilvy lay at Corryburgh the night after the battle - and they went off next morning in a chaise, and asked Him to go with them, but he told them he had been too long already, and that it was only putting off the evil day for 2 or 3 weeks, and starving all that time - and that he was determined to surrender, and throw himself upon the King's mercy. I drank tea yesterday with Lady McIntosh. She is really a very pretty Woman - Pity she is a Rebel. Her sister is a good agreeable Girl. Miss Betty Barber was with her when taken. She introduced me to her. Miss Barber says she knows you...

Kingston's 10th Horse

Historically, regiments of horse were of higher status than dragoons, hence the designation of this provincial regiment raised by the Duke of Kingston specifically for the Jacobite emergency. After the Rising it was re-mustered as the Duke of Cumberland's 15th Dragoons, only to be disbanded in 1748.

The uniform worn by the regiment at Culloden is uncertain. A later painting by David Morier depicts the single breasted red coat appropriate to dragoons with green cuffs and turnbacks, probably derived from Cumberland's livery. At Culloden, however, they are more likely to have been clothed as horse, with full-length lapels on the coat, which like other volunteer regiments raised at this time may have been blue rather than the red worn by regulars. If so the lapels, cuffs and linings will have been red.

Colonel
Evelyn, Duke of Kingston   4 Oct 1745   Not present

Lieut. Colonel
John Mordaunt[4]   4 Oct 1745

Major
Chiverton Hartopp   4 Oct 1745

Captains
Evelyn Chadwick   4 Oct 1745   Lord Robert Manners Sutton   4 Oct 1745
James Otway   20 Mar 1746

Capt. Lieutenant

Charles Hatt	20 Mar 1746		

Lieutenants

Joseph Hall	4 Oct 1745	William Kirke	4 Oct 1745
John Litchfield	4 Oct 1745	Charles Mellish	4 Oct 1745
Nicholas Kirke	20 Mar 1746*		

* Adjutant 4 Oct 1745

Cornets

George Brown	4 Oct 1745	William Hatt	4 Oct 1745
Richard Burton Phillipson	4 Oct 1745	Thomas Smith	4 Oct 1745
Thomas Kirton	5 Oct 1745		
William Paget	20 Mar 1746*		

* Probably not yet joined

Surgeon   John Hall   4 Oct 1745

It would appear that it only mustered 211 troopers at Culloden, which explains why it was deployed in two squadrons of three troops rather than three squadrons of two troops.

Only one man was returned as wounded, but two horses were killed and a third was wounded.

Cumberland's Hussars

Unquestionably the most obscure unit to fight at Culloden, this was a small troop of Germans and Austrians, some 16 strong, which served as Cumberland's personal bodyguard. They were in effect the only genuine Hanoverian troops present.

They wore hussar style uniforms in crimson and green - the Duke's livery. Paintings by Morier and Sandby show a green dolman or jacket with crimson cuffs, worn open over crimson waistcoat and breeches, and a green pelisse slung on the left shoulder. All garments decorated with white cords and lace. A brown fur kolpack was worn, and the pelisse was also edged in brown fur. Morier shows the usual tight Hessian style boots, while Sandby shows dragoon-style high topped boots. Equipment comprised a white carbinbe belt, and a Hungarian style sabre without a knuckle bow. A crimson sabretache, edged white, bore a ducal coronet over a letter W, set within the garter. Saddle housings were crimson, edged white, with the same device as the sabretache.

1 Forbes *Lyon in Mourning* Vol.I : 380-2.
2 *Newcastle Courant* 4-9 May 1746
3 Allardyce, *Historical Papers of the Jacobite Period* Vol.I : 312-14
4 Not to be confused with Sir John Mordaunt, commander of the Fifth Brigade.

The Royal Artillery

The Royal Artillery prided itself on being the most professional of the services - as indeed it had to be - and by way of demonstrating that it took its orders from the Board of Ordnance, its officers and men wore blue coats instead of the traditional red. Its organisation was necessarily looser or rather more flexible than that of the infantry although the basic administrative unit, as in the infantry was still the company. There was no fixed allocation of guns to a company and gunners were expected to be able to serve whatever cannon were deemed appropriate, or at least available, for the job in hand. At Culloden therefore Captain-Lieutenant John Godwin's company was equipped with light 3 pounders, selected for their mobility on Scotland's notoriously bad roads. When the company was afterwards redeployed to Flanders however, they left this particular train of guns in Scotland to be taken over by their successors, while they themselves re-equipped with heavier pieces more suitable to continental warfare.

The numbers of artillerymen present at Culloden are not recorded on the Morning State, although the Guildhall List evidences 1 sergeant, 9 bombardiers, 15 gunners, 67 matrosses and 3 drummers. Uniquely, however, the muster roll for Captain Lieutenant John Godwin's Company survives, recording the names of every artilleryman to serve in it during April - June 1746.

The names are set out in the order they appear on the roll. In total there are 2 sergeants, 12 bombardiers, 27 gunners, 88 matrosses and 3 drummers. Those marked with an asterisk appear to be the men returned as wounded - all of whole subsequently died. Even allowing for these casualties there are still a total of 31 men in excess of the company strength as indicated by the Guildhall List. As they represent a cross-section of all ranks they are clearly not new recruits and so must represent a detachment not present at the battle - probably at Aberdeen.

Captain Lieut.	John Godwin	1 Oct 1745
Lieutenant	Thomas James	1 Apr 1744
2nd Lieutenant	John Cavallier	1 Oct 1745
2nd Lieutenant	William Hussey	1 Mar 1746
Lieutenant Fireworker	Baillie Bryden	8 Apr 1744
	John Worth	12 Apr 1744
	Robert Hinde	2 Oct 1745
	Jasper Leigh Jones	5 Jan 1746
	David Cockram[1]	
Sergeant	Randle Catherall	
Sergeant	Edward Bristoe*	

Bombardier

David McMillan	Samuel Kingsley	Robert Hoult	James Plunkett
James Turner	John Rogers	Thomas Crooks	William Mankin
Thomas Broughton	William Jennings	John Patterson	James Sherwin

These contemporary illustrations depict an officer and gunner of the Royal artillery in blue uniforms with red facings. Note how their lace (gold for officers, plain yellow for gunners) is arranged in a herringbone pattern, rather than the ladder pattern shown in the illustrations of the 13th Foot. (S Reid)

Gunner

Robert Crowe	George Nisbett	Thomas Greenwood	Richard Hammond
Lancelot Usher[2]	John Malman	Thomas Glassup	William Cockup
Thomas Manwaring	Israel Self	Benjamin Ball	John Murdoch
William Parsons	James Smith	James Allen	Thomas Sydenham
Robert Trotter	Thomas Wethered	John Bruce	James Bingley
James Hackett	Abraham Marriot	James Christie	Edward Biggs
Benjamin Godwin	Edward Hurst[3]	John Holdgate	

Matross

Daniel Patterson	Simon Fraser	Lewis Ray	Henry Arnaud*
Robert Cuthbert	William Thomas*	James Lawson	Adam Gray
John Middleton	Lance Carlton	Richard Dessert	Peter Deyman
Thomas Strode	John Strange	John Davison	Richard Hoskins snr
William Partridge	Robert Fern	William Child	Charles Henry
( ) Young	Nicholas Langdon	James Rowland	John Rutledge
Thomas Goodman	William Evans	Robert Fox	Oliver Plunkett
John Wilkins	Michael Morris	Joseph Black	William Moffett
( ) Hamilton	George Skipton	John Rose	Piercy Earle
Charles Grant	John McNeal	Christopher Warrendorf	John Savery
James Sommerville	Andrew Harding	Joseph Brereton	James Butler
Patrick Buchannan	James Donnellan	Thomas Todd	Lancelot Delaney
John Davis	Rowland Davis	John Trinworth	Robert Miller
Thomas Hockley	Nicholas Stevens	Peter Hinkins	Humphrey Houton
Samuel Delamar	John Oake	Murray Gower	Isaac Fennell
George Brown	William Dunkley	William Rider	Francis Dukart
John Sales	Hugh Reynolds	Richard Hoskins jnr	Samuel Chubb*
Richard Faun	Robert Young	John Nicholls	William Shepherd
Thomas Williamson	Amos Hadley	Frederick Bloomer	William Marsh
Edward Ronsall	Henry Deane	William Wallis	William Moore
William Beal	William Harris	Thomas Somerville	Joseph Barnes
John Crone*	Samuel Heywood	John Illingworth*	Mark Young

Drummer

Thomas Dixon	George Guthrie	Francis Naylor

These contemporary illustrations depict an officer and gunner of the Royal artillery in blue uniforms with red facings. Note how their lace (gold for officers, plain yellow for gunners) is arranged in a herringbone pattern, rather than the ladder pattern shown in the illustrations of the 13th Foot. (S Reid)

And Finally...

No-one knows how many women and children followed the British Army to Culloden. There was an official allocation of 6 women per company, which would suggest at least 900 following the regular infantry alone, but they only represented those women carried on the strength for rations, not the many other 'unofficial' women, far less their children.

The Guildhall papers contain the names of the following widows and orphans of sergeants and private soldiers killed at either Falkirk or Culloden:

Hester Mounce (sergeant's widow) and two daughters
Esther Smith, sergeant's widow
Ellen Edge (soldier's widow) and five children
Bridget Moore and two children
Jane Fishborne and one child
Widow Nickle and four children
Widow Cole and two children
Widow Perkins and one child
Widow Richards and two children
Widow Gale and two children
Widow Salisbury
Widow Newsham and three children
Widow Craig and one child
Widow Combes and one child
Widow Wright and four children
Widow Herbert and two children
Widow Bolton
Two orphans of John Johnson
Nineteen other widows of private men belonging to the Glasgow Regiment
Forty-six orphans[4]

1   Sergeant on roll for January-March 1746
2   Promoted to Bombardier after the battle but busted back down again almost immediately
3   Prebble names Hust as a casualty, but this does not appear to be borne out by the roll.
4   The Glasgow Regiment was a provincial volunteer unit which fought at Falkirk.